SIXTIES & S'
DIVERSION DAYS

Part of the 'RINGWAY THROUGH THE DECADES' series

Written and researched by Mark Williams

Published by RINGWAY PUBLICATIONS
www.ringwaypublications.com

RINGWAY PUBLICATIONS

First published in Great Britain 2014

A catalogue record of this book is available from the British Library

ISBN No: 978-0-9570826-6-3

Printed and bound in Great Britain by:
Crossprint Ltd
21 Barry Way
Newport Business Park
Newport
Isle of Wight
PO30 5GY
www.crossprint.co.uk

CONTENTS

	Page
ACKNOWLEDGEMENTS	2
RINGWAY PUBLICATIONS	3
INTRODUCTION	4
SIXTIES DIVERSIONS	5 - 30
SEVENTIES DIVERSIONS – An Overview	31 - 35

SEVENTIES DIVERSIONS

1970	36 - 41
1971	42 - 60
1972	60 - 65
1973	66 - 72
1974	72 - 79
1975	79 - 101
1976	102 - 116
1977	116 - 136
1978	137 - 173
1979	173 - 189

COVERS:

4th November 1971 – Malaysia-Singapore B.707 9M-AOT and Qantas B.707 VH-EAF diverted into Manchester due to a four-day fuel strike at London-Heathrow. (Dave Jones)

ACKNOWLEDGEMENTS

I would like to thank everyone who has contributed by supplying photographs, data, documents, information and encouragement.

I would also like to thank everyone who has visited our historic website, www.ringwaypublications.com from the UK and the rest of the world. Particular thanks go to those who have participated by sharing their memories, stories and photographs.

My eternal gratitude also goes out to:

MANCHESTER AIRPORT ARCHIVE

Michael Hancock, Business Records Officer, for his ongoing helpfulness since 2007, Patsy McClements and the late Paul Isherwood for allowing access to their records since 1994, which included relevant documents, movement sheets, ATC Watch Logs and photographs.

MANCHESTER CENTRAL LIBRARY

The Local Studies Department for arranging ongoing access to their archives since 1992.

PHOTOGRAPH CREDITS

Special thanks go to Geoff Ball for use of his superb collection and also to (in alphabetical order) Ian Barrie, Shaun Connor, Richard Corden, Paul Deakin, Ken Fielding, Michael Gomez, Andy Hall, Peter Hampson, Peter Hardy, John Harrington, Ian Hawkridge, Dave Jones, Dave Lawrence, Neil Lomax, Simon Lowe, Anthony McGhee, MAA Archive, Hubert Parrish, Lloyd Robinson, Gary Shepperd, Barry Swann, Bob Thorpe and Mark White for use of their wonderful photographs.

PROOF READER

Martin Dennett

CONTRIBUTORS/RESEARCH/MOVEMENTS

Geoff Ball, Ian Barrie, Martin Dennett, John Harrington, Dave Jones, Lloyd Robinson and John Wildman. Air-Britain, and former aviation societies such as Centreline/Cheshire Aviation Society/Manchester Aviation Society/PB Enterprises and Manchester Airport Archive for use of their ATC logs.

Mark Williams

RINGWAY PUBLICATIONS

BOOKS:

SEVENTIES RINGWAY 1970 – 1979
EIGHTIES RINGWAY 1980 – 1984
EIGHTIES RINGWAY 1985 - 1989
WOODFORD IN PICTURES
MANCHESTER AIRPORT 75TH ANNIVERSARY 1938 - 2013
SIXTIES RINGWAY 1960 - 1969

Coming next:
NINETIES FOOTBALL, AIRCRAFT ARRIVALS

Forthcoming:
EIGHTIES DIVERSION DAYS
NINETIES DIVERSION DAYS
WOODFORD IN PICTURES 2
CLASSIC JETS
CLASSIC PROPS
MILITARY MANCHESTER
FIFTIES RINGWAY
NINETIES RINGWAY
NOUGHTIES FOOTBALL, AIRCRAFT ARRIVALS

MANCHESTER MOVEMENT DATA CDs/DOWNLOADS:

50 YEARS OF DIVERSIONS MANCHESTER AIRPORT 1960 - 2010
SIXTIES MOVEMENTS
SEVENTIES MOVEMENTS
EIGHTIES MOVEMENTS
NINETIES MOVEMENTS
NOUGHTIES MOVEMENTS

Coming next:
SEVENTIES ATC AUDIO CD, VOL 1

Our books can be purchased from our on-line shop, through our stockists or from any good bookshop.

Visit our historic website coverings all aspects of Manchester Airport:
www.ringwaypublications.com

We can be contacted via our website contact page or by emailing:
info@ringwaypublications.com

INTRODUCTION

During October 1970 when I was seven years old, my family and I moved to Cheadle Heath, Stockport. We lived directly under the flight path of Manchester airport, approximately four miles out on the approach to runway 24. During this time I became very aware of the sound of aircraft passing overhead. Before long I was subconsciously forming a mental timetable of the various sounds, which was easy to do as the airport was fairly quiet at that time of year. At this point I wasn't too interested in seeing or noting the aircraft, but my curiosity was certainly spiked on Sunday 13th December 1970. As Sundays were usually quiet, it was difficult not to notice how noisy and busy the skies were during the morning and early afternoon. I went outside and watched as each 'extra' flight passed over, but at that time they were just noisy shapes in the sky. I tried to make out the colours of each aircraft, but due to their angle it was difficult. The next day at school (Monday 14th December) I noticed it was busy overhead again. Most of the boys at my school were already fully-fledged plane spotters, but at that time my level of interest was not enough to get me started fully. However I had a keen interest in the weather, and began making records about this time, which I still refer to today! It transpired that Manchester handled twenty-one extra flights on the Sunday and twelve on the Monday.

The weather during the last few days of 1970 was cold, with snow becoming more commonplace. By the 2nd January 1971, the airport was experiencing some very cold nights. The following day, Sunday 3rd, was another busy day for overhead aircraft, much busier than the 13th December 1970. I was counting the aircraft by then, and noted there were twenty-one 'extra' flights that day; in fact the exact number of weather diversions was thirty-four. Monday 4th January 1971 was the first day back at school after the Christmas holidays. My typical start to the school day was a twenty minute 'stroll' to school. Since October 1968, the UK had stopped the twice yearly tinkering with the clocks, and British Summer Time was in effect throughout the year. The advantages of not putting the clocks back in October were that it stayed light until much later in the day, and it was not fully dark until around 6.00pm. The downside was that it got light later in the morning, sometimes not fully until around 9.00am, so walks to school were quite often in the dark. Once at school on that particular Monday, there seemed to be a few 'extra' flights. I could hear them from the classroom, but it was after lunchtime about 1.15pm when things went into overdrive. That afternoon in class, on the walk home and once I'd got home, the aircraft never stopped, with one every few minutes. I made a note of a few whilst at home, but the full extent of what happened that day (and during this period of a few days), was not apparent to me until much, much later. The following day there was another buzz from the plane-spotting boys at school over the previous day's events. Although I listened, I did not understand the significance of what they were talking about as it was all new to me. From then on I became an aircraft enthusiast, and have been interested in the subject of aviation for over forty years. It was definitely the 'experience' of January 1971 that got me going, and gave me the passion for the 'the great diversion days of the 1970s', which has stayed with me all this time.

When creating this book, I was very keen to track down existing photographs from this unique period. Thankfully Dave Jones provided me with a number of excellent, high quality images for January 1971. A further unexpected discovery was found buried within the vast archives at Manchester Airport, when I came across more than eighty negatives documenting the evening of the 4th and the morning of the 5th January. These negatives are of varying quality, and I have included a small selection which give a visual overview of the sheer amount of aircraft handled by the airport, and the parking problems they encountered.

Arguably the best period for 'diversions' were the 1970s, in terms of sheer numbers, but the 1980s and 1990s also had great quantities, but the reasons for these arrivals were slowly and subtly changing. By the mid-1990s, aircraft were not necessarily diverting due to not being able to land because of fog for example, it was more to do with not having enough fuel due to holding delays caused by the fog, and restricting the landing numbers. By 2014 fog would still restrict movements at the regional airports, but at the major London airports fog is rarely the reason for a flight to divert. Technology has moved on to such an extent that all passenger aircraft are equipped to land in Cat.III conditions, with a minimum RVR of 200m, with some such as Airbus aircraft able to land with a minimum of RVR of 75m! Such an occasion where the RVR is 50-100m, and remains so for any length of time, is now extremely rare. Reassuring for passengers, but disappointing for enthusiasts!

SIXTIES DIVERSIONS

22nd November 1960 - Interocean Airways Douglas DC-4 LX-IAL diverted in yesterday afternoon, en route from Belfast to Birmingham. The Luxembourg-based airline mainly concentrated on pilgrimage flights, UN relief missions and the transport of gold for the British government. Later they provided aircraft for sub-charters to airlines such as Caledonian and Derby Airways, operating a mixed fleet of Douglas C-54/DC-4/DC-6 and two Carvairs up until their demise in March 1966. (MA Archive via Ringway Publications)

17th February 1961 – Skyways L-749 Constellation G-ANUR is seen on short finals, diverting from Heathrow due to fog, on a trooping flight from Beirut. By 1961, the airline was gradually being run down, and was taken over by Euravia in September 1962. By April 1964 Skyways had disappeared completely. (Hubert Parrish)

9th April 1961 - Pegasus Aviation Vickers Viking G-AHPL had arrived two days previously on a flight from Lyon, originally intended for Blackpool. It is seen here positioning out empty to Tarbes for use on a pilgrimage flight. Operating a total of three Vikings, this was the airlines final year of operation, with its final commercial flight taking place on 25th October 1961. Two days later, all three aircraft (G-AHOY/AHPL/AJBT) departed from Gatwick to Blackpool for storage. (Hubert Parrish)

15th December 1961 – Seen in this late afternoon shot, is recently arrived SAS Douglas DC-7 SE-CCB and BOAC B.707 G-APFJ (BA592 from Los Angeles). In the background is BOAC Britannia G-AOVK and B.707 G-APFI. In the foreground is a 'road' marked out with oil drums, presumably acting as guidance for airport vehicles continuing work on the new terminal and piers. (MA Archive via Ringway Publications).

11th August 1963 – Capitol Airways L-1049G Constellation N4903C arrived at 0003 today from Helsinki as a fuel diversion, and is seen here later in the day parked in the South Bay. It was en route to New York via Shannon, but due to strong headwinds was forced to divert to Ringway. (Hubert Parrish)

17th September 1963 - For a time during the 1960s, US national carrier Pan American used Manchester as their primary UK diversion airport. Today was such an occasion, when four diverted in during the morning. The three seen above are Douglas DC-8 N811PA (PA102 from New York) and B.707s N725PA (PA002 from New York) & N720PA (PA058 from Chicago).
(MA Archive via Ringway Publications)

27th December 1963 - From the 23rd-28th December, Manchester handled seventy-six weather diversions; the bulk of which arrived today. Thirty-two of the thirty-seven flights were from Heathrow, on a day when the record for the most diversions handled in a single day was broken again. Fog in the south was patchy during the day, but it had thickened up by mid-afternoon when most of the diversions arrived. Undoubtedly the pick of these was PIA L-1049H AP-AJZ arriving at 0012, seen above basking in the winter sunshine. This aircraft was deputising for a 'sick' Boeing 720, and departed the following day at 1227 for Karachi via Beirut. In 1969 it was 'donated' to the Indonesian Air Force, serving them until 1973. (Ian Hawkridge)

28th December 1963 - Comet 4 ST-AAW which arrived yesterday at 1713 (SD118 from Rome), was the first visit to Ringway by Sudan Airways. They made five visits during the 1960s with their two Comet 4s (also ST-AAX), with the last on 12th March 1969. In the background is one of three diverted BEA Comet 4s & British Eagle DC-6 G-ARMY. Due to the sheer number of unexpected arrivals, runway 10/28 was closed for the first time and used as a parking area for diverted aircraft. (MA Archive via Ringway Publications)

28th December 1963 – Of the thirty-seven diversions handled yesterday, the only two from BOAC were Boeing 707 G-APFO (BA910 from New York) and G-APFC (BA901 from Beirut), seen parked on pier B with BEA Comet 4 G-APMA (from Moscow) sandwiched in the middle. In contrast to BOAC, BEA diverted eighteen flights into Manchester, including seven Vickers Vanguards (G-APEC/APEH/APEI/APEJ/APEL/ APER/APET). (MA Archive via Ringway Publications)

28th December 1963 - Alitalia SE.210 I-DAXT is seen during the morning, following its arrival yesterday afternoon. Remnants of the old eastern dispersal can still be seen to the left, but this rural scene would be swept away in 1971, when work began on the new international pier and apron.
(MA Archive via Ringway Publications)

5th January 1964 – One of twenty-nine diversions to arrive the previous day, mainly from late afternoon onwards, was KLM Electra PH-LLD (KL135). Disappointingly however, virtually all the Heathrow diversions were British airlines, except for Swissair SE.210 HB-ICU (SR102 from Geneva), MEA Comet 4 OD-ADT (ME213 from Beirut/Geneva), first time visitor Pan American B.707 N760PA (PA100 from New York) and the KLM Electra seen above. (Hubert Parrish).

24th June 1964 – Amongst ten morning weather diversions from Heathrow was BOAC Comet 4 G-APDI (BA937 from Rome), making the first of its two visits to Ringway with BOAC. (Hubert Parrish))

24th June 1964 - Flanked by Heathrow weather diversions BEA Vanguard G-APES & Comet 4 G-APME, Lufthansa Boeing 707 D-ABOD (LH823 from New York) is seen making its first visit to Manchester, taxiing abeam the South Bay having diverted in due to the Heathrow weather. Their passenger-only B.707s would rarely visit Ringway, but in April 1972 Lufthansa inaugurated a twice-weekly B.707F service from Chicago, lasting until October 1973. (Hubert Parrish)

27th September 1964 - British Eagle Britannia G-AOVT 'Enterprise' (from Palma) was the first of two Eagle aircraft to divert from Heathrow, the other being Britannia G-AOVE (also from Palma). This aircraft which would make its final visit to Ringway on 19th August 1968, was sold to Monarch Airlines just prior to British Eagle's collapse in November 1968. In June 1975, it was withdrawn and donated to the Imperial War Museum at Duxford where it still resides today, resplendent in full Monarch colours. (Hubert Parrish)

27th September 1964 – Two shots of Boeing 720 EI-ALA (IN5902 from New York), the first of sixteen weather diversions this morning. One of three operated by Aer Lingus from 1960 to 1972, it would occasionally be seen operating transatlantic charters out of Ringway, or as an aircraft substitution on their European flights. EI-ALA ended its days operating as N1776Q for Aeroamerica from 1974 to 1978, before its withdrawal and subsequent scrapping in 1983. Below the ground engineer is seen descending the aircraft's steps, with the traffic officer and two Manchester Corporation loaders looking on. Another engineer is seen by the tractor, which is towing a diesel ground power unit to provide electrical power to the aircraft. Hitched behind this is an air start unit, which will provide pneumatic air to the engines during start up. The airstart hose appears to be already connected to the aircraft. Notice the ground power unit is in the livery of Manchester Airport Agencies, which later became Servisair. (Both Hubert Parrish)

27th September 1964 - Apart from the occasional charter, BOAC Comets could only be seen at Manchester as weather diversions. G-APDH (11th Dec 1958) was the first to visit on a demonstration flight, and G-APDS (5th Oct 1965) was the last, with many others in between. BOAC Comet 4 G-APDO is seen here returning to Heathrow, having diverted in earlier (BA795 from Istanbul). Also of note parked in the South Bay are three of the six BEA Comets, which had also diverted in during the morning. (Hubert Parrish)

27th September 1964 – Pan American Boeing 707 N767PA (PA002 from New York), was the last diversion from this morning's batch. It is seen here on its first visit to Ringway, flanked by two further Heathrow diversions, British Eagle Britannias G-AOVT & G-AOVE and Spantax DC-7 EC-ATQ which had recently arrived on a charter flight from Palma. (Hubert Parrish)

13

29th September 1964 - Boeing 707 D-ABOC (LH821 from Montreal), was the second Lufthansa B.707 to visit Manchester. This aircraft was the first B.707 to be delivered to Lufthansa in March 1960; serving them until June 1977. Registered as 5A-CVA, it would end its days at Tripoli in the early 1980s, when it was withdrawn and eventually broken up. (Hubert Parrish)

2nd October 1965 – Today's diversion of BOAC B.707 G-ARWD (BA512 from New York) from Heathrow was just one of over 130 diversions during October. Although G-ARWD was only one of seven diversions today, the month would see larger numbers such as the 6th (19), 22nd (19) and 26th (34). (Hubert Parrish)

4th October 1964 – Two British Midland Argonauts seen early on Sunday morning, having diverted in from Birmingham due to fog, are G-ALHG (from Palma) & G-ALHS (from Perpignan). They would depart empty for Birmingham later, after the passengers had been offloaded to leave the airport by coach. (Both Hubert Parrish)

14th December 1965 - Seen in the gathering winter gloom, is Pan American B.707 N763PA (PA101 from Frankfurt), one of two Pan Am flights during the day, with the other being B.707 N727PA (PA056 from Boston). The airport came close to breaking the record for the most diversions handled in a single day, but it did break the record for the most Heathrow diversions in a single day, which was thirty-three.
(MA Archive via Ringway Publications)

14th December 1965 - Qantas B.707 VH-EBB (QF751 from Athens) was one of numerous first time visitors today. Off-duty staff had to be called in to help with the flight chaos, caused by thick fog in the south reducing visibility down to 200yds, whilst Manchester bathed in winter sunshine! Most of these flights terminated at Manchester, with the passengers being taken by surface transport to London. (Hubert Parrish)

14th December 1965 – Two recently arrived BOAC VC-10s are G-ARVK (BA124 from Rome) & G-ARVB (BA272 from Frankfurt). They served BOAC, later British Airways, until 1974 when they were both sold to Gulf Air. (Hubert Parrish)

14th December 1965 – BEA Trident 1 G-ARPR arriving at 1431 (BE'PR from Hamburg), was the penultimate diversion today, joining another three diverted Tridents (G-ARPG/ARPN/ARPW). Amongst the thirty-six diversions were five BEA Vanguards (G-APEB/APEC/APEF/APET/APEU), which can all be seen in the background. (Hubert Parrish)

14th December 1965 - TAP SE.210 Caravelle CS-TCC (TP450 from Lisbon) seen above on its second visit to Ringway, is parked on the east link taxiway. A number of BEA aircraft in the background are parked on the old western taxiway leading to Fairey's. Also amongst today's diversions is D-ABIQ (LH226 from Cologne) below, which is the second Lufthansa Boeing 727 to visit Manchester. Its colour scheme was the airline's classic early-1960s livery, but the titles were slightly different to their other aircraft. However, these variations were discarded, when Lufthansa adopted their classic all blue and yellow tail scheme later in the decade. (Both Hubert Parrish)

14th December 1965 - Due to the sheer numbers of diversions descending on Ringway today, all within an eight hour period, runway 02/20 and various taxiways were used for parking again. However, the lack of parking space coupled with Heathrow's improving weather meant that BEA Trident 1 G-ARPG (BE'PG from Zurich) arriving at 1450 was the last. This general shot looking down pier B towards the aircraft parked on the South Bay, shows South African B.707 ZS-CKC (SA222) & Pan American B.707 N727PA (PA056). (Hubert Parrish)

2nd July 1966 – The first of seven early morning fog diversions produced L-1049H Constellation CF-NAM at 0437 (ND092 from Belfast) as a Stansted diversion. It was the second of two Nordair Connies to visit Ringway. Also of note was the diversion from Heathrow of four British Eagle Britannias in less than two hours (G-AOVB/AOVE/AOVK & ARKA). In April 1969 CF-NAM was sold to CanRelief and ferried to Sao Tome later in the year for use in the Biafran Airlift, but it was stored there by January 1970. Forty-four years later it still sits at Sao Tome in a derelict condition. (Bob Thorpe)

4th November 1966 - Overnight fog covering much of England, southeast of a line from Durham to Dorset during the morning badly affected Heathrow. Twelve diversions and over a thousand passengers arrived during today's session. There was only one first time visitor, with Ghana Airways VC-10 9G-ABO arriving at 1020 (GH702 from Accra/Rome) which can be seen in the background. In the foreground is El Al B.707 4X-ATB which arrived at 0848 (LY252 from New York). (Hubert Parrish)

4th November 1966 – East African Airways Comet 4 5X-AAO (EC716 from Rome) arrived at 1013 and stayed a few hours before returning to Heathrow. In the background is Ghana Airways VC-10 9G-ABO which stayed a little longer. 5X-AAO started life with the airline as VP-KPJ and inaugurated their first jet service from London to Nairobi (EC715) on 17th November 1960. Re-registered as 5X-AAO in April 1964, it served until November 1970, when it was purchased by that great Comet collector, Dan-Air. Unfortunately, it was bought for spares, with a total flying time of 26,224 hours at the time of its arrival at Lasham. It was scrapped in February 1973. (Geoff Ball)

24th November 1966 – Rain last night led to freezing overnight fog in the Midlands and the southeast. All day fog persisted in the south, but it had cleared in most other districts during the morning. Ringway, which was cool and cloudy with medium visibility, had another bumper day of diversions. The bulk of thirty-one arriving from Heathrow mid-morning to mid-afternoon produced a number of first time visitors, including Libyan Arab SE.210 5A-DAB at 1552 (LN105 from Geneva). There were fewer BEA flights than on previous occasions, but BOAC made up for this by sending in B.707s G-APFC/APFN/ARWD/ASZF and VC-10s G-ARVF/ARVK/ASGD & ASGE. (Hubert Parrish)

24th November 1966 - Seen having recently arrived from Heathrow, is South African Airways B.707 ZS-CKD (SA218 from Johannesburg). They operated occasional charters to South Africa and visited Manchester frequently due to bad weather at London. Also in the background are Pan American B.707s N758PA (PA058 from Shannon) & N762PA (PA101 from Frankfurt via Brussels) and Alitalia SE.210 I-DABW (AZ284 from Linate). (MA Archive via Ringway Publications)

23rd September 1967 - Seen on short finals to runway 24, is Britannia G-ANBK (from Barcelona), one of four BKS aircraft diverting in this morning due to fog at Newcastle. The airline operated from Leeds and Newcastle to London and various other points within the UK and Europe. They became Northeast Airlines on 1st November 1970. G-ANBK operated in a temporary colour scheme until it was withdrawn on 31st December 1971, after its final flight from Heathrow to Newcastle (NS442), which was also the last ever flight by a Britannia 102. It was scrapped at Newcastle during March 1972. (Hubert Parrish)

25th April 1968 - Otter CF-XIL (ex 61-423) was one of three ex-Norwegian Air Force examples passing through today, with the others being CF-CDL (64-441) & CF-XJM (ex 5329). They all arrived from Rotterdam and would eventually leave for Shannon, New York and ultimately Manitoba. The departure of CF-CDL was delayed for two days due to a faulty engine, which was convenient for the pilot as he had friends in the area! (Dave Lawrence)

4th January 1969 - Alitalia SE.210 I-DABW (AZA282 from Rome) is seen on Ringway's busiest January day since 1966, when twenty-two diversions arrived in less than five hours, all but one from Heathrow. This particularly foggy 'period' would have fatal consequences, as in the early hours the next morning, Ariana B.727 YA-FAR with 62 people onboard crashed into a house on its approach to Gatwick. (Geoff Ball)

4th January 1969 - Two SAS Douglas DC-9s made their first visits to Manchester today. Seen here is LN-RLK (SK501 from Copenhagen) parked next to Sudan Airways Comet ST-AAW (SD116 from Rome). Due to the bad weather lasting all day in the south, Ringway was running short of space by mid-afternoon and refused to take any more diversions. In Marden, Kent, four people were killed and eleven injured when a passenger train ran into the rear of a parcels train in thick fog. (Geoff Ball)

4ᵗʰ January 1969 – Amongst today's numerous first time visitors was OD-AFA (ME201 from Beirut), on its only visit to Ringway. One of two VC-10s operated by Middle East Airlines, it was delivered new to Laker Airways in January 1968 as G-ARTA, but it never wore their colours as it was immediately sub-leased to MEA. (Geoff Ball)

4ᵗʰ January 1969 - In contrast to the cool, calm and foggy conditions in the south of the country, Manchester had some rain during the morning, which only eased off around lunchtime. This early afternoon shot shows a busy apron. Featured in the South Bay are Alitalia DC-8 I-DIWU, East African VC-10 5Y-ADA and Qantas B.707 VH-EBN, which were all first time visitors. (Geoff Ball)

4th January 1969 - This shot includes more aircraft parked in the South Bay, taken from runway 10/28 this time and with an additional BOAC SVC-10. Six diverted BOAC VC-10 flights today were G-ARVB (BA799 from Tehran), G-ASGF (BA500 from New York), G-ASGI (BA568 from Montreal), G-ASGJ (BA506 from New York), G-ASGL (BA128 from Rome) & G-ASGN (BA130 from Rome). The final diversion on this busy day was also a VC-10 flight, with BUA VC-10 G-ASIW at 1807 (BR662 from Madrid). (Bob Thorpe)

5th January 1969 – MEA VC-10 OD-AFA, which arrived yesterday, is seen being readied for its departure back to Heathrow. Originally the airline had intended to purchase a number of VC-10s, but due to various political pressures, they bought a number of Boeing 707s instead. However, until these were delivered, two VC-10s leased as a stopgap measure were OD-AFA (ex G-ARTA from Laker Airways) & Ghana Airways under-utilised 9G-ABP. The latter aircraft was destroyed in December 1968 at Beirut, but OD-AFA was restored as G-ARTA at the end of January 1969, for operations with British United. (Hubert Parrish)

25

5th January 1969 - Alitalia DC-8 I-DIWU (QZ800 from Pisa) is seen the following day in the Manchester rain. On lease to Zambia Airways, it had been carrying the Zambian President, who was attending a Commonwealth Conference in London. (Hubert Parrish)

5th January 1969 – Still present the following day along with many others, is Sudan Airways Comet 4 ST-AAW (SD116 from Rome), seen here finally being prepared for its return to Heathrow. (Hubert Parrish)

25th February 1969 – Another Sudan Airways Comet, ST-AAX, was amongst the seven weather diversions this morning. It was the penultimate one to visit, arriving at 0819 (SD112 from Rome). The final Sudanese Comet to visit was on the 12th March, again with Comet ST-AAX. It would be another eight years before the African airline came again, by which time they had re-equipped with two Boeing 707s. (Dave Jones)

3rd May 1969 - Morning fog was widespread throughout the Midlands and southern England, where visibility was down to 30 yards. Heathrow and Gatwick were closed for several hours, during which time Ringway received fifteen diversions in five hours. TAP Boeing 727 CS-TBO which made its first visit at 0352 (TP046 from Lisbon), was hurriedly moved to the South Bay in anticipation of more diversions. TAP had operated a fortnightly summer flight to Lisbon in 1965 with L-1049 Constellations, but despite this the airline was still an uncommon visitor to Manchester. (Geoff Ball)

3rd May 1969 - One of several first visits this morning was British Air Services/BKS Trident 1 G-AVYC at 0629 (from Ibiza). They were renamed Northeast Airlines in 1970, but two years later they were devoured by the British Airways amalgamation monster! Also in shot are all three diverted BOAC VC-10s, G-ASGA (BA799 from Beirut), G-ASGD (BA931 from Tehran) & G-ASGG (BA562 from Boston). (Geoff Ball)

3rd May 1969 - Monarch Britannia G-ANCH (OM133 from Valencia) is parked on the western taxiway, which intersected runway 02/20. Purchased by Monarch in 1968, it would go on to serve them until the 30th April 1972, before eventually being flown to Biggin Hill to be broken up there in1973. (Geoff Ball)

3rd May 1969 - Also amongst today's first visits, was Seaboard World CL-44 N124SW, arriving at 0545 (SB124 from New York). With the advent of the airline's introduction into service of their new Douglas DC-8s, this would be one of the aircraft's last flights with Seaboard World, as later in the month it was leased to TMA. In 1971 it was sold to Cargolux as TF-CLA. (Bob Thorpe)

13th August 1969 - SAS 'Sky Freighter' DC-8 OY-KTC (SAS095 from Bergen) arriving at 0705 as a Prestwick diversion, was making its only visit. It was on a regular cargo flight to New York, but scheduled to make an additional stop at Prestwick. It was sold to KLM as PH-DCZ the following year. (Peter Hampson)

20th December 1969 – SE.210 JY-ACT (RJ102 from Amman/Rome) is seen having just diverted from Heathrow, on the first visit of the Jordanian national carrier, ALIA-Royal Jordanian Airlines. This aircraft was one of three operated by the airline, serving them until its sale as HB-ICK in February 1973. It would be a further nine years before the airline visited Ringway again, when B.747 JY-AFA arrived as another Heathrow diversion on 18th January 1978. (Geoff Ball)

SEVENTIES DIVERSIONS, an OVERVIEW

I started making weather records from the age of seven onwards, long before I was logging aircraft. The following has been reproduced from my own notes, and expanded to cover any gaps in my own recordings.

The first three months of 1970 were generally cold, with plenty of sunshine, but snow and hard frosts were commonplace. January 1970 began locally with snow and persistent freezing fog from the 5th to the 7th, but the rest of the month was changeable and very mild at times. On the 28th, fog was widespread in eastern and southern England. February 1970 was sunny, but cold with frequent and prolonged snowfalls in Scotland and northern England. March 1970 was another cold month, which saw the first fortnight and the last five days recording wintry showers or longer periods of snow. There were heavy snowfalls in the south and the 4th saw blizzards hit southern districts. April 1970 began with cold and wintry showers, with periods of snow occurring in most areas at times until the 10th, which was followed by a milder, changeable spell with heavy rain at times. Colder weather returned on the 26th, with more wintry showers.

May 1970 was generally changeable but warmer and drier than average. June 1970 was sunny and warm for the first three weeks, but thunderstorms were also frequent. Manchester had its sunniest June since 1877. It became changeable again across the country for the last ten days, and also into July 1970. The middle of July was very warm but the latter half was unsettled with heavy rain at times. On the evening of the 7th, thunderstorms broke out in southern England, drifting northwards overnight to affect many other areas. These storms produced spectacular and long lasting displays of lightning, which damaged buildings and electricity power installations. August 1970 was warm and dry for the most part, but with occasional thunderstorms that produced some heavy downfalls. The 3rd saw early morning fog, which produced sixteen diversions, mainly from Heathrow.

The first half of September 1970 was locally changeable and stormy at times, chiefly between the 7th and 16th, while the last two weeks were warm and dry. During October 1970 which was generally changeable, fog disrupted flights at Heathrow on several days, including the 8th when ten diversions arrived, and the 18th which produced six which were all BOAC flights. November 1970 was again unsettled, with strong winds and heavy rain at times. Gales were occasionally severe, with the worst day locally being the 3rd. There was also heavy rain leading to flooding at times. Quieter spells of weather were only brief, with one such period being around the 26th when fog was widespread and dense, persisting all day in some places with Heathrow being affected for the most part when Ringway handled twenty diversions.

The first week of December 1970 was unsettled, which led to mainly dry weather until around the 15th. The second half of the month began on a mild note, but after the 21st it became cold with showers or longer periods of snow. Traffic in the south was affected and sporting events on Boxing Day were disrupted or cancelled. Overnight fog, freezing in places, occurring around the 13th to the 15th, affected flights at Heathrow.

Despite the period from the 2nd to the 6th January 1971, when freezing fog occurred widely and lasted all day in places, January was changeable and very mild. During the second week some places had their mildest January day on record. On the 25th a number of whirlwinds were reported in the southeast and a waterspout was observed on the Isle of Wight. Violent winds associated with these phenomena caused local damage. February 1971 was drier than average, but locally there was some heavy rain around the middle of the month. Fog was only a problem on the 11th, when it was particularly dense and slow to clear.

Although there were diversions throughout the next six months into October 1971, they were only bits and pieces and there were no major periods of disruption. March 1971 was changeable with snow showers during the first week and heavy rain during the third week. April 1971 was generally cold and dull but dry, with the third week recording the only rain of the month.

May 1971 was very sunny, with any rain during the month being of a showery nature or with thundery outbreaks mainly around the 25th. After a dry first week, the settled weather broke down and became changeable, with heavy rain for the remainder of the month and below average temperatures. Crops were damaged and swelling rivers disrupted road and rail traffic. July 1971 was sunny and dry for the first three weeks, but the last ten days were unsettled, with thunderstorms or thundery rain. This changeable weather also lasted throughout August 1971, with some very wet and windy periods, accompanied by heavy thunderstorms.

September 1971 was mainly dry with long sunny spells until the fourth week, when low pressure took charge bringing welcome rain to some areas. Apart from the third week which recorded heavy rain at times along with gales, October 1971 was generally dry and sunny by day, but with overnight fog occurring on many occasions. November 1971 was another mainly dry month with lots of sunshine. Mild at first, the weather became colder as the month progressed, with morning fog confined to the first three days and last two days of November, when the fog was freezing and lasted all day in places. The 1st and the 7th December 1971 were foggy days, but on the whole it was a mild month with little sunshine.

January and February 1972 were changeable and dull but generally mild, although there was a cold spell at the end of February that produced a number of fog-induced diversions. March 1972 was stormy during the first week, but from the middle of the month it became more settled. From September 1971 to March 1972, twenty-three Boeing 747s diverted to Manchester, most of which were BOAC aircraft. Apart from the ones in the earlier chapters, Qantas sent in their first, VH-EBC, on 27th February 1972. April 1972 was another changeable month, but more settled from the third week. Worthy of note is the fact that not a single weather diversion arrived into Ringway during this month.

The next three months of May, June and July 1972 were all changeable and cool, with little in the way of prolonged sunshine. However, from the middle of July 1972 there was a sunny and warm spell that led to frequent thunderstorms. August and September 1972 were again cool months, with below average temperatures, but were mainly dry. October 1972 was dry with below average rainfall. November 1972 was generally changeable and although mild during the first week, it became colder during the second week with stormy weather from the 9th to the 13th. Fog persisted all day in some places in southern England and again on the 26th.

December 1972 was a definite tale of two halves. Rain with frequent gales during the first half, but dry and quiet during the latter part of the month, when fog affected many areas from the 17th to the 19th and again from the 28th. Diversions were steady throughout the next few months, with a particularly busy day on Tuesday 19th December 1972, when fifty-two were recorded. This total could have been much higher on the day, but by the evening the airport was struggling to cope with the aircraft already on the ground and had no choice other than to refuse any further flights. This however did not close the year, as in a scenario reminiscent of January 1971; the airport was plunged into chaos again! A persistent fog that lasted over the southern half of the UK for five days from Friday 29th December 1972 until Tuesday 2nd January 1973, recorded 124 diversions. However, the final day of this remarkable period recorded just one diversion, mainly due to congestion on the airfield.

January 1973 was mostly dull but mild, with the only persistent fog being recorded on New Year's Day, covering much of the Midlands and southern England. February 1973 alternated between cold and mild spells, with March 1973 mostly dry with above average temperatures. April 1973 was changeable and cool, whilst May 1973, apart from a few days, was mostly wet with above average rainfall in most parts of England. June, July and August 1973 were mostly dry and sunny, but there were also heavy and thundery rainfalls. September 1973 was warm and sunny at first, before the temperatures started to drop off with heavy rain and thunderstorms by mid-month and generally unsettled thereafter.

The first and last weeks of October 1973 were dry and settled but in between heavy rain, gales and thunderstorms were prevalent. There were numerous diversions from Heathrow on the 26th/28th & 30th, with dense and persistent fog affecting the Midlands and the south during the last week. November 1973 was cold and windy, but often sunny. High pressure dominated the weather during the last ten days, with the 22nd being another day when dense, freezing fog affected the south and more diversions descended on Ringway. The first half of December 1973 was very windy with gales. Mild spells alternated with colder weather, which occasionally brought wintry showers.

In terms of weather diversions, 1974 was a complete disappointment! Although the first few months of the year did see a number of diversion days on the 9th/10th January and the 11th February, the number of arrivals was minimal. The weather pattern at this time was dominated by a continuing series of depressions crossing the country, giving little opportunity for high pressure to become established. However, during early March 1974 an anticyclone became established, and lasted most of the month. It produced some dense and freezing fog in southern England for several mornings around the 20th, which lasted well into the afternoon of the 21st. November 1974 produced a lot of fog in the northwest, but nothing at all further south. Wet, windy and very mild weather was again the feature during December 1974, when Manchester recorded just one weather diversion all month, this being British Airways B.707 G-APFP on the 23rd due to high winds at Prestwick!

1975 began where 1974 left off, lacking in diversions! Despite January 1975 alternating between sunny and cold, or wet and mild weather, the days were generally breezy enough to prevent fog forming. As a result, Manchester only received five diversions during the whole of the month. February 1975 finally produced winter weather susceptible to diversions, with high pressure in charge at the beginning and the end of the month, which produced dry, mild but occasionally foggy weather. September 1975 was exceptionally warm and sunny for the last few days, ending with a series of anticyclones, but prior to this the 8th September recorded a number of Heathrow diversions.

The last few months of 1975 more than made up for the barren spell during 1974. October, November and December 1975 all recorded substantial numbers of extra flights. The last four months of 1975 had been such a bumper period for diversions that one had to question whether it would continue into 1976. Well, the answer to this is that it didn't! Apart from a particularly cold and foggy morning on the 21st February 1976, the rest of the winter would be an anti-climax. In fact, the first few days of the New Year were extremely stormy, causing structural damage locally. Gales affecting the UK on 2nd January 1976 were the most severe for over a century. Manchester airport reported that a number of landing lights were blown over overnight and damaged on the 2nd/3rd. At least twenty-three deaths were recorded, public services were widely disrupted, and the total cost of national damage was estimated at somewhere between £50-100 million.

The alternating cold, mild, and occasionally windy weather would be superseded by the long, hot summer of 1976. It would be long remembered by anyone who lived through it, and it was not without its diversions either. A significant batch arrived on Sunday 29th August 1976, at a time when the continuous pattern of hot weather was showing signs of breaking down. Just a few weeks later, the summer was just a distant memory, when the weather returned into a regular pattern of Atlantic-dominated systems, accompanied by plenty of rain.

October 1976 continued to be changeable, although there were some calmer periods during the month, when fog formed mainly across the eastern side of the country, which saw the resurrection of the 'Leeds' diversion!' Not since the days of BKS and Northeast had there been so many Leeds diversions into Manchester. The month also saw the appearance of Air Anglia at Manchester on a more 'regular' basis. The airline had begun operations from Leeds in 1974 and late 1975, taking over the Amsterdam route from Northeast Airlines. November 1976 was a cold month locally, with plenty of fog during the first half.

When the first visit to Manchester by Concorde took place on the 14th November 1976, the week leading up to it was badly affected by fog, which severely affected operations on the 10th and 12th. December 1976 was also a cold, but generally sunny month, with occasional snow in places, particularly during the latter part when the bulk of the diversions took place.

Cold weather continued into January 1977, but this time there was much more snow around. The heaviest snowfalls occurred from the 10th to the 19th, when deep drifts affected the north and the Midlands. Heathrow was affected on several occasions, as was Leeds during the second half of the month. February 1977 saw Leeds affected on many days, this time by fog. The first major diversion session affecting Heathrow was on 15th February 1977, which fortunately for those at school was during half-term week. Compared to the previous year, the summer weather was unremarkable, and more widely remembered as the 'summer of unrest', due to striking ATC staff in the UK and action by the French and Spanish air traffic controllers, a situation not resolved until early November 1977.

October 1977 was a changeable, with heavy rain, gales and at times above average temperatures, but there was a foggy period across the UK from the 13th to the 22nd. There were numerous road accidents and severe air disruption at Heathrow from the 15th to the 17th. Fourteen cows were killed when a train struck a herd of cattle, which had strayed unseen onto the line near Newark, Notts. The fog was so bad in the Solent, that the Isle of Wight ferries were cancelled for a time.

November and December 1977 were also generally unsettled, mostly mild and very windy at times. By the 13th December, a Scandinavian anticyclone setting up over northern Scotland slowly drifted southeast over the next seven days, and by the 19th it had dense, freezing fog forming under it. Heathrow was closed for most of the day due to the weather. This created some bumper diversion days for airports such as Birmingham, Bournemouth, Cardiff, Luton, Prestwick, Stansted and of course, Manchester.

Although there were periods during 1977 that recorded several days in a row when fog disrupted air travel, such as the 2nd to the 5th January 1971, and the 28th December 1972 to the 1st January 1973, leading to vast quantities of diverted flights; 1978 recorded the most diversions to date within a twelve month calendar year. January 1978 was a very topsy-turvy month, flipping frequently from mild to cold and gales to fog. Whirlwinds recorded as far apart as Hull and Newmarket, caused extensive damage by overturning cars as well as blowing people off their feet! Dense, freezing fog affected the south on the 8th and more significantly on the 18th, when Heathrow was closed all day. In between these dates the country was battered by gale forces, causing further travel chaos on the evening of the 11th when Heathrow was closed for several hours. Northerly gales again affected much of the country on the 28th/29th, but within 24 hours of this fog affected northern England, including Manchester on the evening of the 29th.

There was a very cold spell during the middle two weeks of February 1978, with heavy snowfalls in some areas. More than eighty diverted flights during the month were mainly from Leeds, but others arrived from Liverpool, Birmingham, East Midlands, Blackpool and even Warton and Salmesbury. The pick of these was Venezuelan Air Force C-130 4224, appearing on the 7th February, it was originally destined for Salmesbury with a consignment of Canberra spares.

There were also a number of Heathrow and Gatwick diversions on 21st March 1978, in what had been a fairly uneventful month up until then. It was mild for the first two weeks, but wet and windy for the remainder of the month. April 1978 was changeable with little sunshine and during the middle it became colder with snow showers. May 1978 was ushered in with an extremely cold, dull and miserable day on the 1st, but two days later the conditions became pleasant, warm and sunny, just in time for a number of wide-bodied diversions from Heathrow during the morning. The second part of May was generally dry and very warm. The summer months and into September 1978 could be described cool and changeable, although there was a brief hot spell. The 6th saw Leeds affected by all day fog, which resulted in the arrival of fifteen diversions.

The early part of October 1978 saw high temperatures across the country, when a high pressure established off the southwest and brought very warm southerly winds, which started to break down around the 12th. The following day most of the UK was affected by fog, which was particularly bad in the Midlands, East Anglia and the southeast. The rest of October was cool and breezy and wet at times. The 27th brought dense fog to Manchester airport, which cleared around teatime, but the following day it was Heathrow and Gatwick's turn to be affected by dense fog. The first three weeks of November 1978 were generally mild, but the 10th/11th again brought thick fog to the south of the UK, and severely affected operations at Heathrow and Gatwick. The last week however brought much colder weather with occasional snow.

The UK was hit by wet and windy weather during December 1978, with a few exceptions. Widespread, dense freezing fog on the 4th/5th caused multiple car accidents in eastern England, and affected operations at numerous airports including Leeds and Newcastle in the north, and Heathrow, Luton and Brize Norton in the south. Around the 18th, it became cold again which set up the pattern for the rest of the winter. On the 19th, there were only a handful of arrivals at Manchester, and on the 22nd thick fog again halted operations at Heathrow. Despite a brief mild spell with heavy rain between Christmas and New Year, the cold weather returned with a vengeance as heavy snow swept through the south and the southwest overnight on the 30th.

The New Year was the coldest January since 1963, with frequent snow, and the briefest of mild spells; conditions which continued right through until March 1979. Snowfall was heavy at times, with persistent frosty weather maintaining the snow cover for long periods. There was also occasional drifting in strong easterly winds. Freezing fog added to the travel problems caused by the wintry weather, affecting the south on the 19th and 21st January 1979. On the 4th January, Heathrow was closed for a time due to the extreme cold affecting the ability of the airport to operate safely. Despite all this it was also a very sunny month!

February 1979 was another cold month, although it became milder during the last week. There was further snow, which was heavy and prolonged in some districts. The fresh snow added to the depths already accumulated in January. Considerable drifting in strong easterly winds persisted during the middle part of the month. Freezing fog was also commonplace, resulting in many diversions from a variety of airports. The 25th recorded the highest mean-sea-level pressure of 1045mb since December 1970.

March 1979 was a windy month, and although it was mild at first, it became very cold during the third week with more snow, heavy in parts of northern England and eastern Scotland. April began cold and unsettled with rain, sleet or snow. Mid-month changed towards drier and warmer weather, but this was soon replaced by unsettled conditions again by the end of the month, when it became colder with sleet and snow showers. Although the first four months of 1979 saw some truly appalling weather, it had not delivered the quantity of diversions that the last few months of 1978 had produced.

A deep depression moving eastwards across the country and other troughs sweeping through made the first two weeks of May 1979 a very unsettled period, with showers or longer periods of snow, sleet and rain at times, along with widespread night frosts. The summer months were extremely lean as regards diversions, with June 1979 starting on a very warm note, with a further hot spell from the 17th to the 20th, but otherwise it was unsettled with frequent thunderstorms. July 1979 was mainly dry and became very warm by the end of the month, but with occasional thunderstorms. August 1979 was predominantly changeable and rather cool. Periods of rain or showers were frequent, with thunderstorms again in places. Around mid-month gales occurred over much of England, being particularly severe in the southwest. During the last week of August, there was a spell of more settled weather in many areas.

Much of September 1979, as far as Manchester was concerned, was lost to a fireman's strike. The weather was mainly dry and sunny, but became cooler and unsettled towards the end of the month. October 1979 was typically autumnal, with a lot of fog during the middle of the month, but with periods of wet and windy weather from time to time. The night of the 8th/9th was unusually warm in many areas. Manchester airport recorded a minimum of 16.8°C during the night, which became the highest temperature recorded in any October in the Manchester area since records began in 1877.

November 1979 was predominantly unsettled, with showers or longer periods of rain particularly between the 7th and the 16th. The following day saw a brief respite, with fog affecting the south before another belt of heavy rain passed through the same evening. High pressure became established on the 20th which produced a prolonged period of dense fog, lasting over 48 hours. November ended with another high pressure stretching all the way back to North Africa. The 29th produced some interesting cloud formations and striking colours, which ended with a spectacular sunset. The following morning you could not miss the thin layer of red sand blown up by a Saharan wind, which covered most surfaces and was especially noticeable on cars.

The weather for the final month of the 1970s, December 1979, was unremarkable to begin with, wet and windy for the most part. The second half was very cold, with occasional snow. Heathrow was fogbound for most of Christmas Day, but Manchester did not receive any diversions due to the lack of staff on duty.

SEVENTIES DIVERSIONS

28th January 1970 - The first major diversion session of the decade took place today, with fourteen arrivals during the morning due to fog in the south. Included was South African Airways B.707-344 ZS-SAH (SA234 from Johannesburg/Las Palmas) seen above parked on the end of the domestic pier, alongside Gatwick diversion Caledonian B.707-349C G-AWTK (CA1125 from New York). (Hubert Parrish)

4th March 1970 - Heavy snow across the south and the Midlands brought in a flurry of diverted aircraft during the afternoon. A developing depression moving southeast from the previous evening hit parts of the east and southeast England around lunchtime, where drifting snow blocked roads and brought down telephone and power cables. Operated by Busy Bee of Norway, HS.125 LN-NPC which arrived at 1609 from Milan was originally intended for Heathrow. (Geoff Ball)

4th March 1970 - This is the only visit to Manchester of an MEA CV-990 Coronado. OD-AFK was one of two delivered to airline during 1969, but both had been sold to Modern Air Transport by the end of 1970. It is seen here flanked by two more Heathrow diversions, Austrian Airlines SE.210 OE-LCO (OS451 from Vienna) and Alitalia DC-9-32 I-DIKO (AZ280 from Rome). (Geoff Ball)

4th March 1970 - Another view of the diversions parked on the South Bay. RAF Britannia C1 XL637 'Vega' was a Lyneham diversion (RR6360 from Paris-Orly). Behind are Austrian Airlines Caravelle OE-LCO, MEA CV-990 Coronado OD-AFK and Alitalia DC-9-32 I-DIKO. Today's weather disruption at Heathrow came shortly after an unofficial strike by ninety firemen, which had closed Heathrow for twelve hours from 8pm last night. The dispute was threatening to escalate when a further 3,000 airport employees contemplated joining in. During the twelve-hour closure, BEA announced their timetable had been shattered. They cancelled many flights and diverted others to Luton and Birmingham. International flights were also affected, with departures being rescheduled into the following morning. (Dave Jones)

4th March 1970 - Hansa Jet D-CERA operated by the Singer sewing machine company, is seen parked next to another recently arrived weather diversion, HS.125 LN-NPC. Whilst in the hold at Congleton, D-CERA declared a fuel emergency which threw ATC into further chaos as they were already busy with other inbound diverts, but it eventually landed safely at 1536. Sold in the USA as N300SB in 1973, the aircraft was operated there until 1988, when it was withdrawn. It spent the next six years moving around various locations, before being scrapped, possibly during 1994. (Dave Jones)

4th March 1970 - On a very busy afternoon for flights diverting into Manchester, one of the highlights was the arrival of Aerolineas Argentinas B.707-387B LV-ISC (AR130 from Buenos Aires/Madrid) at 1525. It was the first visit the aircraft and the airline, and it would be another twenty-two years before they would grace Manchester's tarmac again! One of six delivered between 1966 and 1968, it served the airline almost exclusively until its withdrawal in 1992. Parked behind the Argentinas B.707 is another Heathrow snow diversion, B.707-336 G-APFN (BA715 from Frankfurt). In the days before the 'Jumbo' pier and nose-in parking, the scene appears to be a distinctly rural one, although going much further back in time this land was used as aircraft dispersal areas, mainly during and shortly after World War Two. (Dave Jones)

4th March 1970 - As this particular photograph testifies, Manchester also had its share of snow. However, this was accumulated the day before and overnight, before the weather system and all of its snow moved south. Comet 4C SU-ALM (MS771 from Cairo), the first of two United Arab Airlines Comets to arrive during the afternoon, is seen in the South Bay shortly after arrival. (Geoff Ball)

4th March 1970 - United Arab Comet 4C SU-ALL (MS779 from Cairo), the second of two this afternoon, did not stay long before returning to Heathrow. It was on its first visit, but the other, SU-ALM, had already visited on 14th January 1964. Both delivered in 1960, they enabled the airline to extend their route structure to London and later to other European points. Later re-named Egyptair, these aircraft served until 1976 when they were bought by Dan-Air for spares, and destined never to fly again. (Geoff Ball)

13th December 1970 - A large anti-cyclone over the whole of the UK produced quiet, but foggy weather this weekend. Qantas B.707 arrived at 1237 (QF741 from Rome) and a further twenty-one appeared throughout the day including B.707 VH-EAE (QF741 from Rome). Another twelve diversions from Heathrow unusually included three Air France flights, B.727s F-BOJC & F-BPJG and SE.210 F-BHRA. (Hubert Parrish)

13th December 1970 – Douglas DC-9-32 I-DIKI (AZ268 from Rome) was one of two diverted Alitalia flights this afternoon, with the other being DC-9 I-DIKP (AZ284 from Milan). The airline also operated a service

from Manchester in their own right, which commenced in July 1968. For a time from November 1968 to March 1969, they used Douglas DC-9s on their three-times-weekly Caravelle service from Rome/Milan, which extended onwards to serve Dublin. However, by October 1972 aircraft shortages were cited as the reason for ending the four-year service completely. (Hubert Parrish)

18th December 1970 - The morning saw a small, but very interesting collection of diversions into Manchester, with the first two arrivals escaping early morning fog at Dusseldorf. Included was Pacific Western B.707 CF-PWV arriving at 0427 (PW2795 from Montreal) and first time visitor Transavia B.707 PH-TRV at 0555 (HV370 from Vancouver). Another first time visitor was Olympic Airways B.727 SX-CBE arriving at 1053 (OA281 from Athens), which was also the first visit of an Olympic B.727 to Ringway. Also seen here on a grey and misty morning, is East African Airways VC-10 5X-UVJ (EC706 from Entebbe), one of three Heathrow diversions this morning. The airline, East African Airways, was formed in 1946 by four East African governments, Kenya, Tanganika (later Tanzania), Uganda and Zanzibar, all of which were under the rule of the British Empire at the time. Initially operating into Heathrow with Comet 4s, in 1965 the airline placed an order for three VC-10s (5H-MMT, 5X-UVA and 5Y-ADA). Two further aircraft were added, 5X-UVJ in 1969 and 5H-MOG in 1970. However, by 1976 relations between the now three countries (Kenya, Tanzania and Uganda) had begun to deteriorate. Their financial difficulties also deepened, as the latter two countries struggled to pay off their outstanding debts. On 31st January 1977 the operations of East African Airways came to a total halt and they went into liquidation. All three countries eventually established their own independent airlines during the year. The remaining four VC-10s (the fifth 5X-UVA was written off in 1972), were purchased by the RAF and converted to VC-10 K3s for operations as tanker support aircraft. (Dave Jones)

3rd January 1971 – The year began with one of the busiest and most chaotic chapters in the history of Manchester airport to date. The 2nd - 6th produced 107 diversions, mostly from Heathrow and Gatwick (34 on the 3rd and 52 on the 4th). Today's arrivals were the appetiser before the main diversion session the next day. BEA Trident 2E G-AVFK was one of eight different Trident arrivals over the next two days. This along with G-AVFC & G-AVFO would all return for a second time, having made unsuccessful attempts to reach Heathrow. Originally diverting in at 1412 (BE463 from Nicosia), G-AVFK departed for London at 1631 during a temporary improvement in the weather, only to return less than an hour later! (Hubert Parrish)

4th January 1971 - When overnight snow in the south stopped, the mist quickly turned to dense freezing fog, persisting over the blanket of snow. Today's diversions would have been much higher, but there was little European traffic in the skies due to the snow, fog and freezing temperatures there. Arriving within seven minutes of each other today, was first time visitor Boeing 707-331B TWA N18706 (TW6754 from Boston) and TWA B.707 N8737, hot on its heels from Shannon as TW6708. Rather than leave empty back to Heathrow, they departed back to the USA. N18706 as TW8026 to New York and N8737 as TW771 to Chicago, once their passengers had arrived by rail from London. At this point Ringway had only received fifteen diversions, but over the next three hours the airport would see a further thirty-three aircraft crammed into the piers, aprons, taxiways, runway 10/28 and even disused runway 02/20. (Dave Jones)

4th January 1971 - Seen above having just arrived as a Northolt diversion, is USAF Douglas C-118 53-3303, the last of its type based in Europe at the time. Operated by the 7101 ABW at Chievres for HQ SHAPE, it eventually parked on runway 10/28 with Saturn Douglas DC-8 N8955U to keep it company. Below, this late afternoon shot shows of a fully loaded pier B. In the foreground is SX-CBB, one of two Olympic Airways Boeing 727s. (Both Dave Jones)

4th January 1971 - Excluding the Olympic Airways Comets leased to BEA at the end of the 1960s, today saw the first visit of an Olympic Airways flight to Ringway. Boeing 707-348C SX-DBD was the third of three diverted into Manchester by the Greek airline during the day, along with Boeing 727s SX-CBA & SX-CBB. Further diversions to Manchester by the airline took place in October 1971, January 1973, February 1973, and the 22nd December 1978. (Dave Jones)

4th January 1971 - The peak of today's arrivals was from 1400 to 1800, when thirty-five aircraft appeared in the space of four hours, with the eventual total of fifty-two diversions being reached by the evening. It

should also be remembered that most of the preceding day's diverted aircraft were still on the ground at Manchester. Understandably, this caused a great deal of head scratching in the marshallers' office. Seven BOAC VC-10s were parked on runway 02/20, together with various Boeing 707s. Taxiway one between links B and C, and taxiway two between what became links D and E, were subsequently closed and also used for the parking of aircraft. This left link C as the only means of entering and leaving the runway from the apron, with backtracking having to be used. Runway 10/28 was also closed to provide extra parking. In addition to busy times, it was not uncommon to see aircraft 'double parked' on some pier stands. This is the case in the above photograph, which shows BEA Trident 2 G-AVFG (BE605 from Frankfurt) and Caledonian Britannia G-ATNZ (CA1108 from Beauvais) squeezed together on gate 2. Captured in the background is a further BEA Trident, parked up on the Fairey apron. Most of the Caledonian fleet was present during this period, except for three BAC 1-11s, one of which was snowed in at Birmingham. The second was stuck at Liverpool, and the third was grounded in Tenerife. Manchester Airport's director, Mr. Gordon Sweetapple came in for a lot of criticism for handling so many aircraft at once. Services became frightfully overstretched, and with so many thousands of passengers swelling the terminal building, tempers became fraught. However, Mr. Sweetapple made no apology for making Ringway available for the diverted aircraft, and providing them with an airfield to land at. Few airports were open by the afternoon of the 4th, so assisting troubled aircraft in the air was his top priority. At least two Manchester Corporation double decker buses were loaned the airport to ferry passengers from their aircraft to the terminal. A mammoth fleet of coaches, as well as extra trains from Manchester-Piccadilly and Wilmslow, were also made available to ferry the passengers to London. (Dave Jones)

4th January 1971 – This photograph was taken during the evening, when apart from a few exceptions, the airport had finally decided that enough was enough as far as accepting diversions was concerned! Included in the above line-up, is Qantas B.707 VH-EAF (QF743 from Rome) and Caledonian Britannia G-ATNZ (CA1108 from Beauvais). Out of shot and parked in front of the Qantas B.707 was American Flyers DC-8 N123AF. (MA Archive via Ringway Publications)

5th January 1971 – Above, this morning scene shows some of yesterday's arrivals, Olympic B.727 SX-CBA (OA2259 from Athens), SAM SE.210 I-DABV (MQ942 from Rome) and Lufthansa B.737 D-ABEI (LH058 from Cologne). Below, this was the view from the higher tier of the spectator's gallery, above the airport shop. Does anyone remember the 'Manchester Airport Runways Plan'? It was still there in 1975, but had disappeared by the following year. (Both MA Archive via Ringway Publications)

5th January 1971 – Above is a mid-morning view from the ATC control tower. Below, due to parked traffic the options for taxiing aircraft were extremely limited. Departures off runway 24 had to enter further down than normal, due to the NE taxiway leading to the holding point of R.24 being taken up by nine parked aircraft, including Swissair CV-990 HB-ICH & Caledonian Britannia G-ATMA seen here. Out of shot are two BEA Tridents and two B.707s from BOAC & Caledonian. (Both MA Archive via Ringway Publications)

5th January 1971 - These two morning views do not tell the whole story, as every available piece of tarmac able to take an aircraft did so! Most of the previous day's fifty-two diversions were still present at Ringway, but due to an improvement in the London weather, aircraft started to depart from late morning onwards. (Both MA Archive via Ringway Publications)

5th January 1971 – Photographed from inside the domestic pier after diverting in from Leeds is today's sole diversion, Northeast Viscount G-APEX (from Belfast). Although it was painted in an interim Northeast livery with their new tail logo, it still had a BKS fuselage. Eventually all Northeast aircraft would wear an all yellow scheme. The airport was slowly getting back to normal today, following the mass invasion of weather diversions over the last couple of days. (Dave Jones)

11th February 1971 – It was another busy morning for diversions, although most of the twenty-seven were British. TAP Boeing 707-382B CS-TBD (TP450 from Lisbon) which arrived at 1207, marked the first of the airline's 707s to visit Manchester. The airline eventually went on to operate twelve aircraft from 1965 to 1988. In 1986 CS-TBD became the Presidential aircraft of Zaire as 9T-MSS, operating as such for a further ten years. In 1996 it was stored in Lisbon until 2007 when it was scrapped. (Peter Hampson)

11th February 1971 – B.727-30 D-ABIU (LH030 from Frankfurt) as seen above, served Lufthansa until 1978, when it was sold to Aero Peru. The airline had also provided Manchester with the first Boeing 727 visit, when D-ABIC appeared as a Heathrow weather diversion on 7th March 1965. These were part of a twenty-seven aircraft order for the shorter B.727 variant. (Dave Jones)

11th February 1971 – British United VC-10 G-ASIX (BR106 from Nairobi) arriving at 0647, was the first and only Gatwick weather diversion of the morning, the other twenty-six were all from Heathrow! The airline operated the type primarily on their lucrative African routes out of Gatwick, but its identity would totally disappear under the merger with Caledonian by August 1971. (Dave Jones)

23rd September 1971 - G-AWNA (BA506 from New York), which marked the occasion of being the first Boeing 747 to divert into Manchester, was one of only two weather diverts from London. (Hubert Parrish)

3rd October 1971 - Ten days after the first Boeing 747 diverted into Manchester, more bad weather led to the arrival of no less than five Boeing 747s, with four being on the ground at the same time. Included in this batch was the first foreign registered B.747, N93102 (TW700 from New York), followed thirteen minutes later by the first Pan Am aircraft, in the shape of N770PA (PA002 from New York). The other three were BOAC G-AWND at 0952 (BA500 from New York), Aer Lingus EI-ASJ at 1054 (IN2140 from Shannon) and a second TWA, N53116 at 1059 (TW770 from Chicago). The arrival of five B.747s in the space of under three hours led to a few problems on the ground, especially parking space. The first TWA aircraft

(N93102) left before BOAC G-AWND arrived, which helped the situation as the BOAC aircraft parked across the end of the international pier where N93102 had been parked. Pan Am B.747 N770PA had been positioned on the end of the domestic pier on stand 27, which was found to be ideally suited to these aircraft in terms of wingtip clearance. From then on they were used regularly until the completion of pier C in 1974. The arrival of both EI-ASJ & N53116 later in the morning however, meant that parking space had to be found away from the apron, which was already holding a significant number of 'conventional' jets that had also diverted in. The problem was solved by positioning these two aircraft on the southwest taxiway loop over the A538 Wilmslow-Altrincham road tunnel, but this was not the end of the problems. There were only two pairs of B.747 steps available, both belonging to BOAC. Servisair had several pairs of steps which could reach within two feet of the door sill, but they were unsuitable for the offloading of passengers. The outcome of this was that a restriction was placed on the number of 747s which would be initially accepted in a diversion situation. The figure was originally three, but this was raised to seven when the new pier C was opened in March 1974. (Hubert Parrish)

3rd October 1971 - This perfectly timed shot captures three of the five Boeing 747s to divert in during the morning. Seen departing for Heathrow is Pan Am B.747-121 N770PA, while two others, EI-ASJ & N53116, are attracting a considerable number of onlookers. October 1971 proved to be a good month for diversions. Four days later (7th) three more Boeing 747 arrivals were BOAC examples G-AWNB at 1022 (BA506 from New York) & G-AWND at 0913 (BA500 from New York) and first time visitor TWA N93115 at 0950 (TW700 from New York). Other first time visitors during the 7th October were Lufthansa B.707F D-ABUY (LH677 from Anchorage) & Seaboard World DC-8F N8637 at 0419 (SB302 from New York). Finally on the 24th, another ten diversions arrived early morning, and although there was only one Boeing 747, it was another first visit, this time from BOAC B.747 G-AWNG (BA500 from New York). Also of interest on the morning of the 24th was the very early arrival of Boeing 720 OY-DSL (OY261 from Copenhagen) diverting in from Stansted, this being the first visit of the Danish airline, Conair, to Manchester. Also on the 24th was National Airlines DC-8 N109RD again (NA002 from Miami), first time visitor Seaboard World DC-8F N8642 (SB302 from New York), Pan American B.707 N409PA (PA054 from Detroit) and KLM DC-8 PH-DEM (KL6788 from New York). (Dave Jones)

3rd October 1971 - Aer Lingus was one of many airlines that placed an order in the future of air travel, the Boeing 747. Today, the airport received five of the type, and all were first visits. B.747-136 EI-ASJ (EI2140 from Shannon) was one of two aircraft delivered to the airline to operate flights from Dublin and Shannon for their services to New York and Boston. (Dave Jones)

3rd October 1971 – Seen on its first visit to Manchester, is B.747-131 N53116 (TW770 from Chicago). It would divert into Manchester again on the 7th October, on flight TW700 from New York. TWA were regular operators of summer charter flights from Manchester to New York, but were seen only occasionally on diversion here. Shannon remained the airline's weather alternate throughout the 1970s. (Dave Jones)

3rd October 1971 – Above, Pan Am B.747-121 N770PA 'Clipper Great Republic' (PA002 from New York), which arrived at 0839, is parked on the end of the domestic pier. This was Pan Am's first B.747 to arrive at Manchester, and they became regular visitors throughout the 1970s and 1980s until their demise in 1991. Below, Boeing 707-331B N8738 (TW760 from Los Angeles) was one of three TWA aircraft arriving during a busy morning for diversions. The beginning of work on the new International pier can be seen in the background. (Both Hubert Parrish)

4th October 1971 – National Airlines Douglas DC-8-54 N109RD is seen on its first visit, diverting in from Heathrow as NA002. It was one of two, with the other being N108RD, operating their daily London-Miami service until 1972, when they were replaced by Boeing 747s. (Dave Jones)

28th October 1971 - This fine looking Jetstar 731 N3E was en route from Amsterdam-Leeds, but made its first visit diverting into Manchester with technical trouble. It attempted to depart for Leeds on the 1st November, but was beaten again, this time by the Leeds weather! (Ken Fielding)

1ˢᵗ November 1971 - The first few days of November began with a large ridge of high pressure over the southern half of the country, with fog affecting the Midlands, eastern and southern England. Seventeen diversions arriving during the morning from various airports brought in another B.747 first visit! El Al B.747 4X-AXA which arrived at 1022 (LY016 from New York), was the first jumbo delivered to the airline. It also marked the first visit of an El Al B.747 to Ringway. During the early days of the B.747, the airport had no available tow bars, so the aircraft had to park on a taxiway, secondary runway, or on the end of one of the piers as seen here, to facilitate self-manoeuvring. (MA Archive via Ringway Publications)

1ˢᵗ November 1971 - This was the view from the ATC tower around lunchtime. Amongst the aircraft seen in and around the domestic pier are B.747 G-AWNC (BA500 from New York), El Al B.747 4X-AXA and SVC-10 G-ASGD (BA034 from Rome). (MA Archive via Ringway Publications)

1st November 1971 - Pan Am B.747 N732PA (PA002 from New York) is parked on the end of pier B, and British Caledonian VC-10 G-ARTA is nose-in on the South Bay. (MA Archive via Ringway Publications)

1st November 1971 - Dominating this shot are the two Boeing 747s, El Al 4X-AXA (LY016 from New York) and Pan American B.747 N732PA (PA002 from New York). To the right of the Pan American is National DC-8 N109RD and one of the two diverted TWA B.707s. (Geoff Ball)

2ⁿᵈ November 1971 - An official walkout by ground staff at Heathrow the previous day, which lasted until the 4ᵗʰ, saw a number of Heathrow flights call in at Manchester for fuel. B.707 VH-EBR (QF731 Vienna-Heathrow) is seen here having recently arrived. Also arriving during the day were JAL DC-8 JA8037 (JL422 Heathrow-Anchorage) and Syrian Arab SE.210 YK-AFB (RB403 Rome-Heathrow). (Dave Jones)

4ᵗʰ November 1971 - Malaysian-Singapore Airlines B.707-320B 9M-AOT (ML783A Rome-Heathrow) was the last of three fuel diverts this afternoon. The airline (MSA) was formed in 1966 as a result of a joint ownership by the governments of Malaysia and Singapore. They ceased operations in 1972 when both governments set up their own national airlines, Malaysian Airlines and Singapore Airlines respectively. (Peter Hampson)

4th November 1971 – Although taken from a distance, this photograph captures this afternoon's fuel diversions all parked together. Qantas B707s VH-EAF (QF755 from Rome) & VH-EAH (QF735 from Frankfurt) and Malaysian-Singapore B.707 9M-AOT (MI783A from Rome), with the latter two being first time visitors. (Lloyd Robinson)

1st December 1971 – During the first nine days of the month, overnight fog occurred throughout England, mainly affecting the eastern and southern areas, but usually clearing by early morning. This was the case today, but once the sun had gone down the fog reformed and caused chaos in the south. After a batch of morning diversions and a temporary improvement in the Heathrow weather, another twenty-four diversions arrived between 1818 and 2215. One of these is Sobelair SE.210 OO-SBQ, seen above wearing a Ten-Bel logo on the rear of the fuselage. (Geoff Ball).

2nd December 1971 - Nigeria Airways B.707-3F9C 5N-ABJ (WT906 from Lagos/Rome), which had arrived at 1957 the previous evening, was the first aircraft of the West African airline to appear at Manchester. It was one of three different Boeing 707s visiting Ringway between 1971 and 1984, with the others being 5N-ABK (first visit 22nd November 1973) and 5N-ANO (first visit 11th December 1984). One Nigeria Airways flight that did not make it into Manchester was B.707 5N-ABK (WT802 from Lagos) on 15th January 1979. The aircraft had made it as far as Congleton, and was working Manchester Approach on 119.4, when it was advised to re-divert to Liverpool. (Peter Hampson)

27th February 1972 - Six Japan Air Lines DC-8 flights diverting into Ringway from November 1971 to February 1973 with four different aircraft, were JA8010/8012/8014/8037. Today was the only time that two were on the ground together. JA8014 in the foreground arrived at 0813 (JL423 from Anchorage), and JA8012 is taxiing in after landing at 0933 (JL002A from New York) operating JAL's round the world flight. In the early 1970s many national carriers operated these flights, stopping off at a variety of countries. By 1975 the DC-8s had been replaced by Boeing 747s on international passenger routes, although their DC-8s were still seen in the UK, but by then they were operating as freighter aircraft. (Geoff Ball)

18th April 1972 - Early morning fog prevented Cambrian Airways Viscount G-APIM (CS596 from Belfast) from landing at Liverpool, along with fellow Viscount G-AOYJ (CS598 from Belfast). On the 1st April 1972, Cambrian Airways came under the control of the newly formed British Airways Board, and became part of their Regional Division in September 1972. (Lloyd Robinson)

22nd May 1972 - The interesting diversions into Ringway were not always weather-related! Three Bolivian Air Force Convair CV-340s (TAM-41/43/46) were on a ferry flight out of RAF Mildenhall, with TAM 41 being the radio ship for all three aircraft. Still within UK airspace, radio ship TAM-41 developed a problem so all three diverted into Manchester. It is said that the smoke problem in the cockpit had been caused by an engineer leaving an oily rag in the exhaust! Seen above is the second aircraft in the convoy, TAM43, shortly after arrival. (Peter Hampson)

22ⁿᵈ May 1972 – This second shot shows all three Bolivian Air Force Convair CV-340s (TAM-41/43/46) lined up, getting ready to depart. The latter two aircraft, TAM-43 and TAM-46, both crashed in 1993 and 1984 respectively, while TAM-41 was withdrawn and scrapped during the 1980s. (Dave Jones)

22ⁿᵈ August 1972 – Today, Aer Lingus B.747 EI-ASI (IN116 from New York) became the first Boeing 747 to have diverted into Manchester from anywhere other than Heathrow or Gatwick. Although the aircraft arrived on a Tuesday, there were still plenty of spectators to descend on the airport (including myself!), to examine its sheer size at closer quarters. (MA Archive via Ringway Publications)

21ˢᵗ September 1972 – Along with classic vans and fuel bowsers, this shot includes East African VC-10 5H-MOG (EC1752 from Nairobi), Pan American B747 N750PA (PA002 from New York) & TWA B.747 N93117 (TW716 from New York). They were amongst thirteen weather diversions this morning due to fog in the south lasting into the afternoon, which was unusual for this time of year. Also noteworthy were two Boeing 747s parked off the end of the international pier in such a way they could self-manoeuvre off stand. The TWA B.747 is parked well off the pier with two aircraft in the South Bay. Wing tip clearance between these aircraft must have been a close thing, but more of this procedure later in the book! (Hubert Parrish)

17ᵗʰ December 1972 – The month had no wintry weather! The first half was wet with the occasional storm, but this would eventually give way to a large anti-cyclone settled over Europe. The 'benefits' of this quieter weather, was the arrival of sixteen diversions, mainly during the morning. KLM DC-8 PH-DEM (KL6868 from Chicago) is seen parked with BOAC SVC-10 G-ASGI (BA052 from Khartoum). (Hubert Parrish)

17th December 1972 – Qantas B. 707 VH-EAI arriving at 0804 (QF580 from Bermuda) was operating one of the airline's three round the world services. This particular one, The Fiesta Route, operated from 1964-1975, and routed from Australia to Heathrow via Tahiti, Mexico and the Caribbean. (Hubert Parrish)

19th December 1972 – Recently arrived Zambia Airways Douglas DC-8 9J-ABR (QZ800 from Prestwick) is seen in the South Bay. The weather was especially bad, with dense, persistent patches of fog in East Anglia and the southeast, disrupting road, rail and air traffic. Manchester however was relatively mild at 9°C, with six hours of sunshine and North Wales hit a high of 18°C! Making its second appearance in two days was Bahamas World B.707 VP-BDE, along with another new airline to Manchester, Mey-Air, who sent in B.737 LN-MTC at 1356 (MT257 from Roros). After a temporary improvement in the Heathrow weather, another batch of diversions began with BEA Trident 3 G-AWZC at 1536 (BE745 from Zurich). Another sixteen followed in the space of ninety minutes, including two first visits with MEA B.720 OD-AFW at 1608 (ME201 from Beirut) & Zambia Airways DC-8 9J-ABR at 1601 (QZ802 from Prestwick) which had diverted there earlier in the day. Braathens B.737 LN-SUP also arrived at 1620 (BU721 from Gothenburg). The last of fifty-two diversions to arrive on this day was BEA BAC 1-11 G-AVMM at 1816 (BE615 from Berlin), after the airport refused to take anymore due to severe congestion. (Peter Hampson)

20th December 1972 - Seen here parked on runway 10/28 the following morning, are five of the eleven Tridents that arrived the previous day. As more Trident pilots became trained on the Autoland system, scenes like this would become fewer and further between. (Peter Hampson)

30th December 1972 – Singapore Airlines Boeing 707 9V-BBA (SQ785A from Frankfurt) is still wearing the old Malaysian-Singapore Airlines colour scheme, despite the two countries forming their own independent operations earlier in the year. It is seen here parked next to Qantas B.747-238 VH-EBE (QF737 from Rome), the first Qantas B.747 to visit Manchester. In a situation akin to what happened in January 1971, the airport was again stretched to breaking point, due to an unprecedented amount of weather diversions. Sadly, there are very few photos from this period, when from Friday 29th December to Monday 1st January, 123 diversions descended on Ringway. (MA Archive via Ringway Publications).

1st January 1973 – The year started with a further thirty-two diversions arriving on top of the ninety-one received over the last three days of 1972. Seen here on a gloomy afternoon are Olympic Boeing 720s SX-DBG & SX-DBK, having diverted from Heathrow as OA259 & OA281 respectively. Amongst the aircraft in the background are Pan American B.707 N404PA (PA054), which arrived the previous evening and JAL Douglas DC-8 JA-8037 which arrived late morning as JL423 from Anchorage. (Geoff Ball)

2nd January 1973 - During the previous day, Manchester handled an extra 3,000 passengers. Airports such as Liverpool, Birmingham and Gatwick also benefitted from an extra influx of passengers, and income! On a much brighter day than yesterday, seen here are KLM DC-8 PH-DEE and MEA Boeing 720 OD-AFW making its second visit in less than a fortnight. (Peter Hampson).

2nd January 1973 – Featured in the shot above is Pan American B.707 N404PA and the penultimate National Airlines DC-8 to visit Manchester, N108RD. The DC-10 seen departing in the background was Laker Airways DC-10 G-AZZC, a Gatwick diversion from last night. Note that unusually all three aircraft in the South Bay are parked nose-in. Featured below is Syrian Arab SE.210 YK-AFC (RB405 from Damascus/Rome). Arriving at 2301 the previous evening, this was the airline's second Caravelle to visit Manchester. BOAC B.747 G-AWNI (BA437 from Munich) seen in the background, held for over four hours in the south awaiting a clearance in the Heathrow weather, before eventually diverting to Ringway. The day had similarities to two years earlier, when on the 4th January 1971, Manchester was the only major airport open, and under great pressure to handle vast amounts of diversions. This time round however, the airport showed more restraint, by turning away at least thirty diversions. (Both Peter Hampson)

4th February 1973 - From January to March 1973, ten 747s diverted into Manchester. The most notable was the first visit of a South African Airways B.747, with the arrival of ZS-SAO (SA234 from Johannesburg/Frankfurt). However, things went far from smooth for this aircraft! It is seen above on the through taxiway at the end of international pier, stuck between BOAC B.747 G-AWNK on stand 11, and a BOAC Super VC-10 parked on the South Bay, which resulted in a considerable delay for ZS-SAO. Seemingly related to this event, South African Airways gave Manchester the 'diversional cold shoulder' for the next two and a half years, preferring to use Prestwick instead. (Geoff Ball)

4th February 1973 - South African Airways B.747 ZS-SAO (SA234 from Johannesburg/Frankfurt) is seen again here, but this time at its eventual spot, possibly stand 47 adjacent to the end of the domestic pier. All five of the airline's Boeing 747-244Bs would visit once Manchester was back in favour. They even diverted in a couple of their Boeing 747SPs during the 1980s. (Lloyd Robinson)

4th February 1973 - Japan Air Lines Douglas DC-8s were not uncommon to Ringway during the early 1970s. Seen with work on the new international pier and multi-storey car park going on in the background, today's appearance of JA8014 (JL411 from Tokyo/Copenhagen) was the final JAL DC-8 to visit Manchester. It would be nearly two years before the next JAL visit, when B.747 JA8122 arrived on 30th November 1975. (MA Archive via Ringway Publications)

11th March 1973 - One of three Heathrow fog diversions during the morning was Swissair DC-8 HB-IDB arriving at 0731 (SR2163 from New York). In 1973, European airlines were still able to operate transatlantic flights via Heathrow, but these would be outlawed by the end of the decade. (Peter Hampson)

29th August 1973 - Five wide-bodied jets on the ground at once broke the previous record set on 3rd October 1971. All are captured in this shot taken from the tower building. The four B.747s are G-AWNC (BA500 from New York), G-AWNM (BA024 from Nairobi), Pan American N747PA (PA120 from Los Angeles) & TWA N53110 (TW700 from New York). The fifth wide-body, Laker DC-10 G-AZZC, which is operating Manchester's weekly Toronto flight, is parked on the end of pier B.
(MA Archive via Ringway Publications)

29th August 1973 – This morning's diversions brought in an extra 2,000 passengers for the airport to cope with, on top of dealing with their own passengers within a terminal already bursting at the seams! Both TWA B.747 N53110 (TW700 from New York) & B.707 N762TW (TW754 from New York) were first time visitors. TWA, like South African Airways, would also have parking issues with their B.747s, which had an impact on their diversions into Manchester. (MA Archive via Ringway Publications)

22ʳᵈ November 1973 – Two of three BOAC Boeing 747s to divert in during the morning are seen in this shot. Huddled around the end of pier B is G-AWNI (BA026 from Frankfurt) & G-AWNC (BA664 from Miami). Also note that although Manchester did not have any B.747 operations at this point, BOAC had already invested in steps for the aircraft, in preparation for events like today. (Geoff Ball)

23ʳᵈ November 1973 - Yesterday produced twenty-five fog diversions, mainly from Heathrow. Although it was predominantly a British affair again, it did produce the first visit of Nigeria Airway's newest Boeing 707, 5N-ABK, seen in the background. The busiest period was late evening, when fourteen Heathrow diversions arrived from 2217 to 2349. Incidentally, Birmingham received at least twenty-five BEA diversions during the evening, including sixteen Tridents. The three Tridents seen here are Trident 3 G-AYVF and Trident 1s G-ARPH & G-ARPZ, all with new British Airways titles, but still in BEA colours. (Geoff Ball)

71

24th December 1973 - The formation of British Airways in 1974 also meant that Cambrian Airways would disappear, although their 'CS' flight-codes would remain for another two years. Seen on a crisp and sunny Christmas Eve, is BAC 1-11 G-AVOE (CS678 from Heathrow), one of five late morning Liverpool diversions due to fog. (Anthony McGhee)

21st March 1974 – TWA Boeing 747 N93104 was the first foreign-registered jumbo diversion into Manchester in 1974. The aircraft, which arrived at 0743 today as TW700 from New York, was originally

parked on stand 12 on the end of pier B. This stand was found to be suitable for the nose-in parking of B.747s and other wide-bodied types following the introduction of nose-in parking in November 1972. After a rapid refuel, the aircraft taxied out to the holding point, but severe air traffic control delays into the London TMA prevented its departure for at least an hour. Whilst N93104 was burning precious fuel at the holding point, BOAC B.747 G-AWNF (BA817 from Rome) arrived and parked on stand 12. With ATC forecasting delays of several hours into London, the TWA captain decided to return to stand 12, but unfortunately this stand was now taken. The TWA B.747 was then marshalled onto stand 23 as seen above, on the new international pier C. By parking there, it became the first wide-bodied aircraft to use the new apron. Customs would not allow the air bridges to be used, as they were still to approve the new pier, so aircraft steps were used instead. The exact situation regarding the air bridges occurred again four days later on 25th March 1974, when BOAC B.747 G-AWNN (BA506 from New York) arrived on the official opening day of the airport's new buildings. It was painted in British Airways brand new colours, but again this aircraft also had to use aircraft steps instead of the air bridges. (Hubert Parrish)

21st March 1974 – An interesting view of the aircraft, taken from the end of the domestic pier. In the foreground is BEA/British Airways Trident 1 G-ARPG (BE5015 from Glasgow), whilst in the background parked on the South Bay is East African Airways VC-10 5Y-ADA (EC634 from Frankfurt), along with various other British Airways Group aircraft sporting their various liveries. The aircraft above seen in new colours are B.707 G-APFP and SVC-10 G-ASGM. In fact at this point, the airline still had a long way to go in terms of painting their aircraft into the new corporate colours. Five years later the odd Boeing 747 could still be seen sporting the classic BOAC livery and several Tridents were also noted in old BEA colours, but with British Airways titles. (Geoff Ball)

21st March 1974 – All but one of this morning's twelve diversions arriving between 0743 and 1043 were from Heathrow. Seen here is HB-ICE (SR800 from Zurich), which was the last diversion of the day and the final visit of a Swissair CV-990 to Manchester. All eight operated by the airline had been sold by 1975, with most being purchased by the Spanish airline, Spantax. (Hubert Parrish)

21st March 1974 – Aircraft were now parking nose-in to the pier. This scene shows a number of this morning's diversions, including British Caledonian B.707 G-AZJM (BR222 from New York) and Zambia DC-8 9J-ABR (QZ802 from Lusaka/Rome). Newly arrived BOAC B.707 G-APFM (BA556 from Chicago) is seen passing the end of pier B, where two of Manchester's own transatlantic services, VC-10 G-ARVJ (BA538/7) & B.707 G-APFJ (BA648/9), are also parked. (Geoff Ball)

25th March 1974 – Police marksmen and army bomb disposal experts were called this morning, after special branch detectives uncovered an IRA bomb plot, following a swoop on a suspect's home. The security operation involving more than 200 police was ordered when detectives found plans of the new extension, maps and drawings with hand written comments on them during the raid. While the security operation was taking place, one of several weather diversions was Boeing 707 JY-ADP (RJ001 from Washington), arriving at 0941 due to fog at RAF Brize Norton. This was King Hussein of Jordan's aircraft, stopping off in Britain for a brief visit. The King remained onboard until security had cleared the way for him, and twenty minutes later he was hustled away by detectives and his fifteen bodyguards to a private suite at the airport for refreshments. He stayed for ninety minutes, before departing for London for talks with his ambassador. Today's other major event was the official opening of the airport's new £8.3m extension. Manchester became Britain's first drive-in airport, almost double its original size, capable of taking the biggest airliners with loads of up to 400 passengers. With the capacity for 5 million passengers a year, it would also be able to cope with 4,000 passengers an hour at peak times, a figure equal to the total number using Ringway airport annually before the Second World War! The new extension had doubled the size of the control tower administration block, which housed ATC and new departments such as telecommunications and meteorology/aeronautical information services. There was also a new thirteen level multi-storey car park, a check-in hall with fifty desks, a baggage handling system, an immigration and customs hall and an international arrivals area. The new intercontinental pier C for long-haul passengers was now connected to the terminal building by moving walkways, equipped with air bridges linking directly to the aircraft. Pier C was now capable of taking up to four B.747s and one B.707 or VC-10, or seven B.707/VC-10s. The airside frontage of the existing terminal building had been extended outward by 30ft and international departures now has a transit lounge restaurant, cocktail bar, private dining suite and roof terraces. The old customs hall now converted into an extension of the main concourse area, gives an additional waiting area and the western half of the booking hall has been adapted as a domestic baggage claims area. The domestic and international piers were now known as A and B respectively. (MA Archive via Ringway Publications)

25th March 1974 - The city's Lord Mayor officially opened the airport's £8.3m extension today. Despite builders' strikes and a shortage of materials, it still took less than five years from design to completion. Also the final cost was close to the original estimate. It was slightly unfortunate that the first two aircraft to park on the airport's brand new pier C were both diversions! On the left, King Hussein of Jordan's entourage are seen disembarking into a police van, whilst parked next to it is British Airways B.747 G-AWNN (BA506 from New York) with more than 250 passengers. Note that both aircraft are parked away from the air bridges, and are using steps instead. (MA Archive via Ringway Publications)

26th March 1974 – A morning diversion from Stansted, Pacific Western B.707 C-FPWJ (PW523 from Montreal), was noted in the airlines new colours. It was the first Canadian aircraft to visit Manchester with the recently adopted C-, rather than CF-. Another morning arrival was Heathrow diversion TWA B.707F N15713 at 0720 (TW609 from Frankfurt), which was also a first time visitor. (Ken Fielding)

29th April 1974 - Eight diversions arriving during the morning due to fog, included VH-EAB (QF007 from Bombay), which became the final visit to Manchester of a Qantas B.707. Twenty-five different Qantas Boeing 707s had visited since the first, VH-EBC (16th September 1963), as either diversions or operating emigration/families charters. The Australian airline was in the process of phasing out the type on its European services, before eventually becoming an all-B.747 service. (Ken Fielding)

29ᵗʰ April 1974 - On a dull and misty Monday morning, British Airways B.747-136 G-AWNC (BA018 from Nairobi) is seen about to position onto the end of pier B (stand 14, side on). This aircraft was the first 'Jumbo' to arrive at Manchester, back on the 17ᵗʰ August 1970. (Hubert Parrish)

29ᵗʰ April 1974 – TWA N770TW (TWA754 from Boston) kept its passengers onboard during the morning, pending an improvement in the weather. (Hubert Parrish)

14th May 1974 - Belgian Air Force Douglas DC-6 OT-CDF/KY-4 is seen having just arrived at Manchester en route Woodford-Brussels as a technical diversion. This aircraft saw sixteen years continuous service, before being sold to SFAir as F-BYCJ in January 1977. (Geoff Ball)

10th February 1975 – Fog was said to have affected thirty counties in England and Scotland during the day. There were many collisions on the roads and motorways, which involved some fatal accidents.

Ringway escaped the worst of it, although it remained dull throughout. Seen here are B.747 G-AWNP, Alitalia DC-9 I-DIKL (AZ282 from Rome), SAS DC-9 OY-KGO (SK511 from Oslo) and BEA Airtours B.707 G-ARWD (KT061 from Ottawa). The writer knew nothing of today's diversions, due to low cloud preventing any views of the flight path from his school in Heaton Norris! (MA Archive via Ringway Publications)

10ᵗʰ February 1975 – Today was the best day for diversions for quite some time. The thirty-one arrivals due to fog were mainly from the southeast. Included was British Airways latest B.747, G-AWNP, making its first visit to Manchester (BA510 from New York). This aircraft was one of nineteen diverted flights from British Airways throughout the day. (MA Archive via Ringway Publications)

23rd February 1975 – B.747 G-AWNP (BA560 from Boston) is seen paying another visit, alongside B.707s G-APFC & G-ARRA, operating Manchester's New York & Toronto flights respectively. Snow had been absent so far this winter, but today it fell briefly in the south, resulting in several Heathrow diversions during the morning. One that got away however, was Air India B.747 VT-EBE (AI112 from New York), which would have been the first visit of Air India since B.707 VT-DNZ on 18th September 1971. It was holding at Barton, and despite an ongoing strike by Servisair who handled the airline at Manchester, special arrangements had been made between the management and staff to accept the aircraft; but by this time the Heathrow weather had improved and the B.747 decided to go there instead! (Geoff Ball)

10th May 1975 – Zambia Airways made their first visit to Ringway since March 1974, with this morning's early arrival of B.707 9J-ADY (QZ'DY from Lusaka). Seen above returning to Heathrow, this aircraft was relatively new to the airline, having been recently purchased from Aer Lingus (ex-EI-ASN). (Geoff Ball)

8th September 1975 – Of the ten diversions arriving during the morning, all but two were from British Airways. Two of the aircraft seen here, B.707 G-ARRC (BA440 from Montreal) and B.747 G-AWNO (BA941 from Montreal), were Heathrow diversions. (Geoff Ball)

17th October 1975 - Alitalia B.747 I-DEMO (EI8214 from Prestwick) had carried out a charter from Rome to Dublin and was due to position to Prestwick to pick up some passengers for Rome. Dublin had been foggy for most of the day, and by the time it was due to depart, the Prestwick visibility had fallen below limits. It was eventually decided to send the aircraft to Manchester to pick up its Scottish passengers and bring over several hundred people from Dublin who had been stranded by the bad weather. (Geoff Ball)

24th October 1975 - A ridge of high pressure centred over Scandinavia, drifting towards the southwest, resulted in calm, sunny, but very foggy conditions. Over the next six days seventy-one weather diversions descended on Manchester. The day had started fairly innocuously with one early morning diversion, British Airways BAC 1-11 G-BBME (BE883 from Rome), but by 0930 the flood gates had opened! British Airways G-AWNP (BA610 from Montreal) seen above, was one of two BA B.747 arrivals this morning, with the other being G-AWNH (BA660 from Miami). (Peter Hampson)

24th October 1975 – East African Airways VC-10 5Y-ADA (EC644 from Nairobi) was one of twenty diversions today, arriving between 0949 and 1108. It was making the last of its three visits to Manchester. (MA Archive via Ringway Publications)

24th October 1975 - Lufthansa flights destined for Heathrow made rare diversionary visits to Manchester, usually opting to divert to Gatwick or make the return back to Germany. Today however saw one of those rare exceptions, when B.737 D-ABCE (LH056 from Cologne) seen here and B.727s D-ABKB (LH040 from Hamburg) & D-ABKI (LH030 from Frankfurt) all ventured north! (Ken Fielding)

24th October 1975 – Due to this morning's influx, the South Bay was filling up with diverted aircraft. Seen parked next to KLM DC-8 PH-DEA (KL119 from Amsterdam), is Luxair SE.210 LX-LGF (LG401 from Luxembourg), making the aircraft's and the airline's first visit to Manchester. (Peter Hampson)

24th October 1975 - From 1950 to 1990, Pan Am operated an extensive network of scheduled services between West Germany and West Berlin, as a result of an agreement reached between the USA, UK, France and the Soviet Union at the end of WW2. This prohibited Germany from having its own airlines and restricted the provision of commercial air services from/to Berlin to airlines from these four countries (Air France/BEA/Pan Am & Aeroflot). Pan Am would also introduce services between various points in Germany to Heathrow, in order to feed their transatlantic passengers onto flights from Heathrow. B.727 N326PA (PA055A from Hanover) became the first such flight to divert into Manchester. (Ken Fielding)

24th October 1975 – N580RA from Milan, which became the eleventh different Gulfstream 2 to visit Manchester since the first in September 1969, was also the first of its type seen by the writer. It is parked on the South Bay, next to Lufthansa B.727 D-ABKI, which was also a first time visitor. (Peter Hampson)

24th October 1975 - Alitalia DC-8 I-DIWG (AZ458 from Milan), was the penultimate diversion of this particular session, witnessed by the writer at home while enjoying his lunchtime spaghetti on toast! It had first visited in October 1971, and would make one final visit on 15th December 1975. (Peter Hampson)

28th October 1975 - Only four days after the last major diversions session, further fog caused havoc on the UK's roads and airports. For those of us still at school, the half-term holidays were perfectly timed for these diversion days! British Airways B.747s G-AWNC (BA437 from Tel Aviv) and G-AWNH (BA3500 from New York) which is still in old BOAC colours, are seen basking in the morning sunshine. (Geoff Ball)

28th October 1975 – B.707 9Y-TEK (BW900 from Port of Spain) was making the first visit to Manchester of British West Indian Airlines (BWIA). Earlier in the year the Caribbean airline had commenced operations into London with four ex-Northwest Orient Boeing 707s. These were operated until 1980, when they were replaced with four Lockheed L.1011-500s. (Ken Fielding)

28th October 1975 – Manchester seemed to be back in favour with South African Airways following the February 1973 incident! B.747 ZS-SAM (SA234 from Johannesburg/Sal Island) has recently arrived, and is seen amidst a seemingly empty apron. This aircraft was carrying a spare engine under its port wing, an occasional practice around this time. (Peter Hampson)

28ᵗʰ October 1975 – Pacific Western C-130 CF-PWK (PW386 from Ankara) arrived in the early hours as a Stansted diversion. In 1968, the airline operated several C-130s flights from Manchester, transporting computer equipment to various destinations. CF-PWK, which was making its only visit, was written off in April 1982, after catching fire whilst unloading gasoline at a remote location in Canada. (Geoff Ball)

28ᵗʰ October 1975 – Monarch Airlines were uncommon visitors to Manchester in 1975, seen only occasionally operating ad hoc charters or as diversions. They had recently replaced their Bristol Britannias with BAC 1-11s, and G-BCXR (OM439 from Palermo) seen here parked on taxiway 2 was one of three early morning Luton diversions. (Ken Fielding)

28th October 1975 - Another diversion, B.707 G-BDKE (BR6478 from Lagos), is seen parked on runway 10/28 in basic Qantas colours and British Caledonian titles. Operating on a short-term lease to BCAL since the end of September 1975, it returned to Qantas as VH-EAC in early-1976. (Ken Fielding)

29th October 1975 - Fog in the south again mainly affected Luton and Gatwick. IAS Cargo DC-8 N8782R (FF502 from Lagos) had arrived last night after a temporary improvement in the weather during daylight hours. Originally delivered to Trans Caribbean Airlines in June 1963, it was bought by IAS in 1975. It was initially operated with its US registration, before becoming G-BDHA in February 1976. In 1979 the airline merged with Stansted-based Transmeridian, to form the short-lived British Cargo Airlines. (Ken Fielding)

29th October 1975 – Slow to clear fog in eastern areas, lasted all day in parts of Lincolnshire, Yorkshire and the Midlands. Six Britannia Airways B.737s were present on the international pier on this day and ten different aircraft had diverted into Manchester during a 24 hour period over the 28th/29th. Liverpool was also affected by fog, and was the reason for the appearance of Eli Lilly Corporation Boeing 707 N309EL, as seen above, looking a little shabby! (Ken Fielding)

14th November 1975 – Dense, freezing fog across eastern England for the last few days, developed more widely over the UK in the early hours. It affected Heathrow well into afternoon, and produced eleven diversions to Manchester, six of which were first time visitors. Malaysian Airlines made their first visit since the split of Malaysia-Singapore Airlines, and B.707 9M-MCS (MH894 from Kuwait) seen parked on stand 21, departed direct to Kuala Lumpur via Kuwait the following evening as MH893D. (Ken Fielding)

14th November 1975 – Malaysian and Singapore Airlines had operated as the combined airline, MSA, until 1972, but ironically today saw both airlines divert into Ringway for the first time as their separate identities. Singapore B.707 9V-BDC (SQ743A from Frankfurt) is seen on its first visit parked next to another first time visitor, TWA B.707 N8733 (TW754 from Boston). (Lloyd Robinson)

14th November 1975 - Pan Am B.747 N738PA (PA002 from New York), another first time visitor to Manchester, eventually positioned out later in the afternoon to Frankfurt. This shot was taken prior to the arrival of Qantas B.747 VH-EBD, which would park on stand 24. (Geoff Ball)

14th November 1975 – Iran Air was another airline making its first visit. In 1975 they operated a three-times-weekly Tehran-New York service via Heathrow (IR777), returning in the opposite direction the next day. B.707 EP-IRN (IR776 from New York), which was making the first of only two visits by the Iranian airline, is seen parked on the end of pier B next to B.747 G-AWNK (BA510 from New York). However, during 1976-1977, Iranian Air Force Boeing 707 aircraft were regularly seen at Ringway. (Ken Fielding)

14th November 1975 – The penultimate Heathrow diversion this morning, was Qantas B.747 VH-EBD 'City of Perth' (QF001 from Frankfurt), which positioned out to Heathrow the following morning. It served the airline from 1971-1980, and operated its final flight on 14th February 1980 prior to withdrawal and onward sale to Eastern Airlines, having flown 31,791 hours and 10,297 cycles. However, the sale was not taken up, and the aircraft returned to service and operated for a further five years. (Ken Fielding)

14th November 1975 - Taken from quite a distance, this shot captures four Boeing 747s on a sunny Friday morning (VH-EBD/N738PA/G-AWNO & G-AWNK). Disappointingly, the diversions had dried up by mid-morning, probably due to British Airways' ongoing handling issues. Gatwick handled a large number of Heathrow diversions, and by late afternoon they were full to capacity. Over 1,500 passengers from the diverted aircraft were dealt with at Manchester, before being railed to London - eventually! Several more diversions arrived from the Midlands early evening, just as fog started to descend on Manchester, but due to low pressure sweeping across the country, it did not last long. (MA Archive via Ringway Publications)

30th November 1975 - This Sunday morning shot taken from the domestic pier, captures last night's arrivals. Of the thirty-one appearing between 2021 and 2359, all but eight were diversions. Fog affecting central, southern and eastern England again, disrupted coastal shipping, road and air travel. On the evening of the 29th, ten people were killed in two separate light aircraft crashes. One was at Birmingham and the second at Elstree claimed the life of Formula One racing driver, Graham Hill. (Geoff Ball)

30th November 1975 - Transmeridian CL-44 G-AZIN (KK557 from Dubai) was one of last night's arrivals, having been unable to land at Stansted. Purchased by the airline from Flying Tigers in 1971, it was subsequently leased to British Air Ferries from 1971-1973, and is still in basic BAF colours. (Geoff Ball)

30th November 1975 – TWA B.707 N18706 (TW702 from New York) was another of last evenings arrivals. Now sporting the airline's new colours, this was the second of its two visits to Ringway. Although it was very misty at times during the weekend, Manchester escaped the worst of the dense, freezing fog which lasted until late evening. (Geoff Ball)

30th November 1975 – Wardair B.707 C-FZYP (WD402 from Vancouver), was another arrival during a busy morning period, which saw twelve diversions between 1001 and 1142. This aircraft departed in the early hours of December 1st as WD803 to Toronto. (Geoff Ball)

30th November 1975 – The only airline operating Ilyushin Il-62s into Manchester at this point was Tarom, so the arrival of SP-LAC (LO341 from Warsaw) broke that sequence! It is seen here still in old colours, having recently arrived from Warsaw on diversion from Heathrow. Note the four aircraft (Laker B.707s G-AVZZ & G-AWDG, BCAL B.707 G-AZJM and British Airways B.707 G-AXXZ) clustered together parked on the old southwest taxiway. Il-62 SP-LAC positioned out in the evening to Warsaw. (Geoff Ball)

30th November 1975 – Swissair DC-9-51 HB-ISM (SR810 from Geneva) was the first 'stretched DC-9' to visit Manchester. The airline would begin using DC-9-51s on their Manchester-Zurich service from June 1981, replacing their DC-9-32s. (Geoff Ball)

30th November 1975 – JAL B.747 JA-8122 (JL411 from Tokyo/Copenhagen) is seen taxiing to stand 25 with British Airways B.707 G-ATZD (BA240 from Nassau) in the foreground. The 24 ILS was unavailable during the day, so from a personal perspective, it appeared to be making a spectacular visual approach, turning onto the approach around six miles out, which I saw from my high-rise flat. It operated out late evening as JL412 to Tokyo via Copenhagen, once its passengers had arrived from Heathrow. (Geoff Ball)

30th November 1975 – BWIA B.707 9Y-TEE (BW900 from Bridgetown) was the second to visit Ringway. Once the airline had introduced their L.1011 Tristars, they would continue to use Manchester as one of their main diversion airports. However, after the arrival of 9Y-TGN on 27th November 1982, it would be a further seven years before the airline was seen at Manchester again. (Geoff Ball)

30th November 1975 – RAF XV101 (RR2495 from Akrotiri) is seen having recently arrived, positioning itself onto stand 26. There would be a temporary improvement in the London weather by late afternoon, but it fell below limits again around teatime, when two further Heathrow diversions arrived. The first was Kuwait Airways B.707 9K-ACU making its first visit at 1842 (KU181 from Rome), and the second was Nigeria Airways B.707 5N-ABJ at 2014 (WT914 from Rome). (Bob Thorpe)

30th November 1975 – There had been moderate frost overnight, which lasted all day on the parts of the apron that saw no sunlight. Singapore Airlines B.707 9V-BFW (SQ765A from Zurich), which was the second to visit Ringway, served the airline until 1981 by which time it had been replaced by Boeing 747s on their European services. It departed the following afternoon back to Heathrow as SQ736. (Geoff Ball)

30th November 1975 - Tunis Air made their first visit to Ringway today, with B.727 TS-JHO (TU790 from Tunis). It is seen here, having arrived earlier in the day as another Heathrow diversion. This was another flight that operated direct from Manchester once its passengers had been coached up from London, departing at 2003 as TU791 back to Tunis. (Geoff Ball)

30th November 1975 – A fantastic shot of three diverted Alitalia Douglas DC-9s. Front to back, last night's arrival I-DIKT (AZ292 from Milan) and today's arrivals, I-DIBO (AZ282 from Rome) & I-DIKE (AZ8216 from Milan). Aircraft turned away by Ringway today due to handling problems or ground congestion, were Qantas B.747 VH-EBG (QF001), EL AL B.707 (LY315) & MEA B.720 (ME201). (Geoff Ball)

15th December 1975 – Air New Zealand DC-10 ZK-NZN (BA598 from Los Angeles) which had been holding at Pole Hill beacon, decided to divert to Gatwick. However, by the time he was southbound approaching Honiley beacon, he was told that Gatwick was full after accepting diversions all morning. He did a 180° turn and proceeded to divert to Prestwick, but on his way north he heard B.747 G-AWNL (BA941) en route Prestwick-Heathrow hoping in vain for a clearance in the London weather, but soon after he requested a diversion to Manchester instead. The pilot of the Air New Zealand DC-10 decided to follow suit, and by doing so, made first visit of the airline to Manchester. (Peter Hampson)

15th December 1975 - Heathrow remained below limits for most landing aircraft all day and into the following morning, but this diversion day was slow to start! Low cloud and 200m visibility restricted movements at Ringway during the morning, but the fog soon cleared. It remained dull and there were only three diversions until midday. However, the arrival at 1402 of first time visitor Singapore B.747 9V-SIB (SQ773A from Frankfurt) was one of a steady stream, which continued into the evening. Also in shot are British Airways B.747s G-BBPU (BA600 from Montreal) and G-AWNI (BA881 from Tehran). (Geoff Ball)

16th December 1975 – Yesterday's fog at Heathrow was bad enough to prevent the return of Manchester's diversions back to Heathrow. Nigeria Airways B.707 5N-ABJ is seen being repositioned onto a stand. Aircraft in the background include B.747s G-AWNL & G-BBPU, VC-10s A4O-VK & G-ARVM and Saudi Air Force C-130H 462, which ironically was also a Heathrow diversion. (Geoff Ball)

16th December 1975 - Seen parked next to Qantas B.747 VH-EBD, is recently arrived TWA B.747 N93108 (TW760 from Los Angeles), one of four diversions this morning, despite Manchester having a visibility of 150m in fog. The other three diversions were also TWA aircraft, with first time visitor B.707 N18707 (TW1756 from Philadelphia) plus B.707 N28727 (TW6754 from Boston) and B.747 N93104 (TWA700 from New York). (Geoff Ball)

16th December 1975 - Gulf Air VC-10 A4O-VK has now been re-positioned onto stand 14, whilst Qantas B.747 VH-EBD is seen taxiing for departure back to Heathrow. The VC-10 would leave late evening direct for Dubai as GF016, once its passengers had arrived from Heathrow. (Geoff Ball)

21st February 1976 – On a dull Saturday morning, a brief ridge of high pressure calmed the weather down temporarily. Twelve early morning diversions included Braathens B.737 LN-SUP, which departed back to Malmo once the passengers had arrived from Stansted. East African VC-10 5H-MMT (EC654 from Athens) is seen here parked next to another diversion, British Airways B.707 G-AXGW (BA560 from Boston). (Paul Deakin)

21st February 1976 – Bangladesh Biman came into existence shortly after the country's independence in 1972. They received their first Boeing 707, S2-ABM, the following year when the airline began services to London-Heathrow. Their second B.707, S2-ABN, was delivered at the end of 1973 and is seen here making the first visit to Manchester of both the aircraft and the airline. (Paul Deakin)

21st February 1976 – This shot shows Laker Airways B.707 G-AWDG parked on domestic gate 50, despite having arrived from New York, along with two Dan-Air Comets; G-AYVS on an eight-day layover and G-BDIF (DA1717 from Nuremberg) as a Gatwick diversion. In the foreground is RAF VC-10 XV105 parked on gate 48 (RR2024 from Bahrain), which offloaded its troops and bags for onward transportation back to RAF Brize Norton. (Paul Deakin)

1st August 1976 - Arriving on a very warm but cloudy Sunday afternoon with engine trouble, is Cessna 182 N44CC from Zurich, which left later in the evening bound for Prestwick. (Geoff Ball)

2nd August 1976 – One of the best movements of the year was the only visit of a Royal Saudi Air Force Jetstar, 101. Arriving at Manchester on the 28th July from Riyadh via Rome, it was a day later than originally planned. After attempting to leave on the 31st July, it returned ninety minutes later as an emergency technical diversion with fuel pump trouble. It sat on the South Bay for a further five days, before finally departing on the 5th August as seen below. (Above Lloyd Robinson, below Geoff Ball)

29th August 1976 - In the midst of a long hot summer, dense fog in the southeast provided Ringway with twenty-one London diversions. Seen amongst the aircraft cluttered on the South Bay and runway 10/28 is Gulf Air VC-10 A4O-VG (GF121 from Dhahran), flanked by British Caledonian B.707 G-ATZC (BR2706 from Los Angeles) and British Airways B.707 G-ATWV (BA478 from Montreal/Prestwick). (Neil Lomax)

29th August 1976 - CP Air DC-8 C-FCPT in the foreground was not a diversion, but the photograph is included for the aircraft in the background. Of the eleven wide-bodied jets arriving during the morning, ten were on the ground at the same time, which created a new record. Diversions in such quantities were uncommon for August, and the last time this happened was in 1973, which coincidentally was also on the 29th August! Most of today's diversions, which were mostly long-haul, left late afternoon and into early evening due to the crews going 'out of hours'. (Geoff Ball)

29ᵗʰ August 1976 – Included in this shot of diverted aircraft parked on the old runway 02/20, now taxiway C, are three British Airways Boeing 747s; G-AWND (BA500 from New York), G-AWNI (BA560 from Boston) still in full BOAC colours but BA titles, and G-AWNO (BA0660 from Miami). B.707 G-AYLT is seen on departure, operating BA539 Prestwick/New York. (Geoff Ball)

29ᵗʰ August 1976 – National Airlines had recently replaced DC-8s with Douglas DC-10s on their NA002/1 Heathrow-Miami service. DC-10 N82NA, which had arrived during the morning on its first visit to Manchester, is seen taxiing for departure back to Heathrow. (Geoff Ball)

29ᵗʰ August 1976 - Seen being repositioned from runway 10/28 onto a stand on pier C, is Pan American B.747 N657PA (PA002 from New York), which made its first visit to Manchester today. The hot summer of 1976 finally came to the end the following day, when a belt of rain sweeping through the country was the first significant rain in many places for three months. (Geoff Ball)

29ᵗʰ August 1976 – Seen here are SVC-10s G-ASGC (BA861 from Dubai), G-ASGE (BA080 from Paris) and G-ASGH (BA090 from Nairobi) on stand 23. Often ignored by spotters on diversion days, the British Airways Super VC-10s could sometimes be the indicator of weather diversions. Once our New York and Toronto services had arrived, other British Airways SVC-10s outside of these times were uncommon; so the sound of one of these magnificent machines on a misty winter's afternoon or evening was not to be taken for granted! (Geoff Ball)

14th November 1976 – The event of the year was the first Concorde to arrive at Manchester. Diverting from Heathrow due to fog, G-BOAA (BA578 from Washington) touched down at 2138, having decided that holding further south was futile. Once inside UK airspace off southern Ireland, it routed northeast towards Brecon then Barton for a landing on runway 24. (MA Archive via Ringway Publications)

15th November 1976 – The morning after the night before! Several airport workers had to stop to admire this magnificent aircraft, parked up on stand 14. (Lloyd Robinson)

15th November 1976 – What must the passengers on the Britannia Airways B.737 made of the aircraft parked on the stand next door? This shot was taken before thousands of spectators descended on the airport. In contrast the photograph below shows the situation several hours later, once word had got round! Despite it being a weekday, the surrounding roads were choked with cars heading towards Ringway and pier B was soon closed off due to the sheer numbers. (Above Lloyd Robinson, below Michael Gomez)

15th November 1976 – Gulf Air VC-10 A4O-VK (GF121 from Bahrain) was an early morning diversion, so it was hopeful there would be more. However, there were only three further arrivals from Heathrow during the morning, despite Heathrow still being affected by dense fog up until lunchtime. (Anthony McGhee)

15th November 1976 – British Airways B.707 G-AXGX (BA560 from Boston) and B.747s G-AWNE (BA510 from New York) & G-BDPV (BA600 from Toronto), were the final Heathrow diversions until the fog thickened up again late afternoon. This led to a further six diversions from 1700 to 1800, including the first visit of a Lufthansa Airbus A300, with the arrival of D-AIAB (LH034 from Frankfurt). (Anthony McGhee)

15ᵗʰ November 1976 – Over the past few days Manchester had been at a virtual standstill due to fog, but today the east of the UK was affected by the worst of the weather. Air Anglia G-BDVS (AQ200 from Norwich) was one of five Leeds diversions during the morning. (Anthony McGhee)

15ᵗʰ November 1976 – The cold and crisp morning winter sunshine had by now been replaced by grey and misty weather, eventually giving way to wind and rain. TWA B.707 N773TW (TW702 from New York), which made its only visit to Manchester today, was one of the ten late evening diversions from the previous night. It is seen here during the afternoon on its return to Heathrow. (Anthony McGhee)

15th November 1976 - British Airways L.1011 G-BBAI (BE745 from Copenhagen) became only the second to divert into Manchester, despite their numerous visits during late-1974 and early-1975 on 'extended' flight training duties. Prior to their eventual revenue service in January 1975, the Tristar was the cause of several industrial disputes at Heathrow, mainly over new working practices. (Anthony McGhee)

15th November 1976 - Gulfstream 2 N200A, operated by the Mobil Corporation and a frequent visitor to Heathrow at this time, had also arrived the previous evening with four passengers on a flight from Gander. Although the Gulfstream 2 had been around since 1966 and had become a common type at Heathrow, N200A was only the eighteenth to visit Manchester since the first, N902, arrived on 16th September 1969. (Anthony McGhee)

15th November 1976 - British Airways Concorde G-BOAA is seen taxiing to the R.24 hold past a collection of light aircraft parked on the freight apron. Included is Robertson Foods PA-31 G-OLLY and Bass Charrington's Cessna 401 G-AYOU. Last night's Concorde passengers were initially held onboard pending a possible improvement in the Heathrow weather, but they were offloaded when the pilots and the company realised no improvement was imminent. Some chose to spend the night at the Excelsior Hotel, and others completed their onwards journey to London on a specially chartered train. (Anthony McGhee)

18th November 1976 – Air Anglia Fokker F.27 PH-ARO (AQ201 from Edinburgh), had been recently leased by the airline from Fokker, and was still in the livery of its previous operator, Linair. It returned to Fokker in October 1977, and was sold on to Belgian International Air Services. It was then leased to Air Anglia again, this time as G-BFDS, before finally returning to B.I.A.S in November 1978. (Geoff Ball)

13th December 1976 - There was a distinct lack of sunshine at Manchester this month, and today was no exception. On a very murky morning, Malaysian Airlines B.707 9M-MCR made its first visit to Ringway, arriving at 1019 (MH894 from Kuwait). Another Heathrow diversion of interest today was Simbair Boeing 707 5X-UWM, operating East African Airways flight (EC556 from Cairo). The latter airline was in desperate financial trouble, and finally ceased trading in February 1977. (Geoff Ball)

23rd December 1976 - British Airways Concorde G-BOAA made its second visit to Manchester at 1158 (BA301 from Bahrain), due to fog at Heathrow. In the background is IAS Boeing 707 G-BEAF (FF333 from Cairo) which had recently arrived as Gatwick diversion. (MA Archive via Ringway Publications)

29ᵗʰ December 1976 - The year ended on a cold, but sunny note under a large ridge of high pressure. This produced another diversion session during the morning, albeit a brief one! Another BWIA Boeing 707 first time visitor was produced, with 9Y-TEK (BW900 from Port of Spain). Also parked on the international pier are Qantas B.747 VH-EBE and British Airways B.747 G-BBPU (BA520 from Washington). B.707 9Y-TEK departed later in the morning with the intention of returning to Heathrow, but due to landing delays and no significant improvement in the weather, it ended up diverting again, this time into Gatwick. (Geoff Ball)

29ᵗʰ December 1976 - The second first time visitor of the morning was South African Airways B.747 ZS-SAN 'Lebombo' (SA226 from Sal Island). This aircraft was also forced to divert to Gatwick due to the Heathrow weather and ATC delays. (Geoff Ball)

29th December 1976 – Of the seven Heathrow diversions to arrive, four of these were Boeing 747s. Included was TWA B.747 N93107 at 0655 (TW760 from Los Angeles) on its first visit to Manchester and Qantas Boeing 747 VH-EBE (QF007 from Bombay) at 0714 on its second visit. (Geoff Ball)

11th January 1977 – Warton diversion, French Air Force Nord 262 No. 86, was due to depart the following day, but it developed an unserviceable starboard engine. French Air Force MS.760 Paris No.53 was dispatched from Villacoublay with the necessary spare parts, but by the time the Nord 262 was ready to go on the 13th, Ringway had closed due to snow, but it managed to depart before midnight. (Geoff Ball)

13th January 1977 - G-BOAD (BA301 from Bahrain) was the third Concorde flight to divert into Ringway in as many months, but today's arrival was also a first visit. Heathrow had been suffering from snow showers up to the point of its arrival, but it diverted in for fuel due to lengthy holding delays caused by single runway operations. By mid-afternoon it was Manchester's turn to be affected by the weather, when numerous flights were diverted away. (Peter Hampson)

14th February 1977 – One of seven Leeds diversions during the day was Schreiner Airways PA-31-350 PH-SAV, making the first of two visits while Dutch registered. In 2006, it was purchased by Norwich based operator Skydrift, still wearing basic Schreiner colours thirty years later! (Geoff Ball)

15th February 1977 - The second day into my week-long half-term holiday from school produced a healthy batch of morning diversions into Manchester. The fact that the weather had calmed down enough to produce any fog at all was a real surprise, as the weather up until this point had been mainly wet and very windy. Unusually for me, I got out of bed later than usual, and it was 8am before I finally turned my aircraft radio on. Having already looked out of the 7th floor window of my bedroom, it seemed rather gloomy, with the cloud base quite low. I soon realised how low the cloud was when I heard an aircraft go over, but I could not see it. Generally I would have been able to see the aircraft at around five miles from touchdown and about 2,000ft, but that was not the case today. After switching on my radio, I was an excited schoolboy on hearing British Airways B.747 G-AWNJ 'Speedbird 889' calling up on Tower 118.7. On the approach frequency was National Airlines DC-10 N82NA (NA002 from Miami), and two more BA 747s not far behind were G-AWNI (BA520 from Washington) & G-AWNA (BA660 from Miami). Unfortunately, I was up too late for the following diversions which had arrived earlier, British AW SVC-10 G-ASGP at 0733 operating as MK042 for Air Mauritius, TIA DC-8 N4868T at 0758 and British Midland B.707 G-AYVE at 0828 (KQ114 from Nairobi). Seen in this shot is recently arrived Ghana Airways VC-10 9G-ABO (GH702 from Rome), making its first visit to Manchester since September 1975. Some of the others during the morning included British Airways Trident 3 G-AWYZ (Shuttle 713 from Edinburgh) due to the captain not being Cat.III authorised and Swissair DC-9-51 HB-ISO (SR800 from Zurich), which was on its way to Birmingham when their RVR fell below limits. Most aircraft enthusiasts by now would have been getting on their bikes, or getting out their bus fares for a trip to the airport. My preference however was to do the opposite and stay at home for two reasons. Firstly, I lived on the flight path in a high-rise flat and it was unusual for me to miss anything. Secondly, I liked to tune into the radio and listen in to what was diverting where, in the hope I would pick up flights not normally heard and monitor what was likely to be coming into Manchester. Although I was sorely tempted to try and cadge some bus fare off my mum and catch the 369 to the airport as I could not see anything because of the low cloud, I decided against it and recorded some audio instead. (Garry Shepperd)

15th February 1977 - The star movement and last diversion of the day, was Thai DC-8 HS-TGZ 'Thai International 900', arriving at 1058 from Bangkok via Athens. It was the first lander I had seen all morning, as it broke through the clouds at just the right moment. Sounding very impressive on the radio, it would be another twelve years before Thai visited Manchester again. It departed empty to Heathrow during the evening. (Above Peter Hampson, below Geoff Ball)

15th February 1977 – The audio I recorded from Sudan Airways B.707 ST-AFA, which arrived at 1008 (SD112 from Rome), had a very loud whine in the background. The conversation from the pilot was almost inaudible and would not be allowed by ATC nowadays. Seen in the background is one of two diverted Lufthansa aircraft during the morning, B.737 D-ABEM (LH040 from Hamburg), with the other being D-ABGE (LH056 from Cologne). (Garry Shepperd)

15th February 1977 – This photo taken around lunchtime from the ATC tower shows a very busy scene for a Tuesday in February! Apart from the numerous diversions, also of note is Laker Airways Boeing 707 G-AWDG parked on the domestic pier on gate 48, despite it arriving on a scheduled flight from Toronto (GK7132). (MA Archive via Ringway Publications)

7th March 1977 - A short-lived colonial diversion session affecting approximately 1,000 passengers produced an interesting selection. Included was the first appearance of Air Jamaica, with the arrival of DC-8 6Y-JII at 0735 (JM002 from Kingston); and first time visitors Qantas B.747 VH-EBG (QF007 from Bombay) & National DC-10 N83NA (NA002 from Miami) which is seen above. Other arrivals were Gulf Air VC-10 A4O-VK (GF121 from Dubai), South African Airways B.747 ZS-SAL (SA258 from Sal Island) & British Airways B.747 G-BDPV (BA600 from Toronto). (Geoff Ball)

12th March 1977 – This colourful aircraft, Aerostar N300AM, aborted its attempt on a round-the-world speed record after developing technical trouble. It was a first visit of type, arriving at 1538 en route Gander-Frankfurt after being forced to divert in with low oil pressure. It left after receiving two hours attention on the South Side. (Geoff Ball)

15th October 1977 - Qantas B.747 VH-EBD (QF007 from Bombay), which was making the second of three visits during the decade, is seen returning to Heathrow less than two hours after its arrival. This aircraft made a further two diversionary visits during the early 1980s, before its withdrawal on 21st March 1985 and subsequent sale. (Geoff Ball)

16th October 1977 - The air traffic control watch log recorded at 0330, "The barriers would be removed from disused runway 02/20 due to the prospect of possible diversions from the south". It transpired that a total of thirty-nine would appear during the day, thirteen of which arrived before 0700, when Heathrow and Gatwick were both below landing limits due to fog. The figure could have been higher, had Manchester not been affected by fog. Although it never fell below limits, it was bad enough to restrict diversions from 0700 to 0900, when only two arrived. Leased Gulf Air L.1011 N81027 seen here arriving at 0910 (GF1027 from Dubai), started the next wave of diversions, when seventeen arrived within ninety minutes. (Geoff Ball)

16th October 1977 – Following closely behind the Gulf Air L.1011, was first time visitor Air India B.747 VT-EDU (AI112 from New York), making the airlines first appearance at Manchester since 1971. Two further diverted flights during the month were VT-EBE on the 17th (AI116 from New York) & VT-EBD on the 25th (AI102 from New York). (Geoff Ball)

16th October 1977 – Dan-Air B.707 G-AZTG (KM102D from Malta) arriving at 0921, had been on lease to Air Malta during the summer. Curiously, it carried Dan-Air titles and Air Malta colours on the starboard side, and full Air Malta colours on the port side. (MA Archive via Ringway Publications)

16th October 1977 - CP Air DC-8 C-FCPL arrived at 0934 (CP816 from Toronto) but is seen leaving the South Bay on its return to Gatwick. Also in shot is British Caledonian B.707 G-BDLM (BR682 from Tenerife). In the background parked on runway 28 is Zambia Airways B.707 9J-ADY (QZ924 from Lusaka). (Shaun Connor)

16th October 1977 – The second of two British Airways B.747 arrivals this morning, G-AWNJ (BA500 from New York), is seen here leaving for Heathrow. (Shaun Connor)

16th October 1977 – Once a regular to Ringway, BA Cargo Boeing 707F G-ATWV (BA969 from Dubai), made its penultimate appearance, and is seen being repositioned onto the South Bay. It stopped visiting when British Airways dropped their final cargo service through Manchester earlier in the year. (Shaun Connor)

16th October 1977 – Air India B.747 (AI112 from New York) landed at a time when the Manchester visibility was around 800m. Seen parked side on to gate 14, it held its passengers onboard pending an improvement in the Heathrow weather. (Barry Swann)

16th October 1977 – Although the aircraft in the foreground, United Biscuits Beech 200 G-HLUB, was not a diversion, this shot shows how packed the South Bay and runway 28 had become with diverted aircraft. By early evening another session was threatening, when the Midlands and later the southeast were affected by fog. By the time Jetstar N40XY arrived at 2100 as a Luton diversion, Manchester was also affected, and to such an extent that its own flights were diverted away. (Geoff Ball)

16th October 1977 - Gulf Air VC-10 A4O-VG arrived at 1432 (BA1242 from Heathrow), and stayed for a ninety-minute technical stop, before continuing its flight to Prestwick. Note that the aircraft operated under a British Airways call-sign with its Gulf Air titles painted out. At this time the airline was in the process of phasing out their VC-10 fleet. (Shaun Connor)

16th October 1977 – Two shots of Trans Europa SE.210 EC-CIZ (TR240 from Palma), which diverted into Manchester at 1133 today due to the East Midlands weather. Although the Spanish charter airline had been in existence since 1965, they only operated regular IT flights from Ringway between 1976 and 1981. (Above Shaun Connor, below Geoff Ball)

16th October 1977 - Another diversion day when the tally could have been much higher, as both Heathrow and Gatwick were below limits all morning - but so was Manchester! By midday, Ringway's weather had improved enough to accept diversions. Seen above is Gatwick diversion ONA Douglas DC-8 N866F (OV866 from New York), terminating at Manchester after offloading its passengers. Amongst today's first time visitors was Qantas B.747 VH-EBA (QF007 from Frankfurt) and Air India B.747 VT-EBE (AI116 from New York). Aer Lingus B.707 EI-ASO overshot at 1344 (IN6015 from Chicago) on diversion into Manchester, operating a Dan-Air flight with a Shamrock call-sign. It got to 2-miles final, when its company gave instructions to overshoot and proceed to Gatwick instead. Fog affecting Birmingham, Luton and Gatwick send in further diversions during the evening. (MA Archive via Ringway Publications)

2nd December 1977 – Boeing 727 G-BFGN, which arrived last night at 2257, was wearing basic Delta colours but no titles. It was on delivery, en route Goose Bay-Gatwick, when it diverted into Manchester due to strong headwinds. (Geoff Ball)

16th December 1977 – IFA Douglas DC-6 OO-IFA (ex-Air Djibouti) arrived at 0012 from Frankfurt, transporting car parts on behalf of Ford. Manchester had been handling an increased number of cargo flights originally destined for Liverpool, but due to a firemen's strike they were re-routed to operate via Ringway instead. Newly formed this year, the Belgian airline made their first revenue flight on the 16th June 1977, taking eighty-six passengers from Brussels to Jersey. They also operated cargo flights, after fitting a cargo door during a major overhaul in 1975. Arriving in a stylish orange and blue livery, this was the aircraft's only visit, as the airline ceased trading in May 1978, and it was sold as N799TA. (Peter Hardy)

19th December 1977 - Today's major diversion session produced some interesting aircraft. This late-morning shot shows a small selection of the arrivals so far. Some local fog earlier on was beginning to clear, by the time the first divert arrived, which was South African Airways B.747 ZS-SAM at 0702 (SA234 from Johannesburg/Sal Island). It was missed by the writer, as it was the first day of the school holidays and there was no rush to be up early. Although I was up and about by 8am, once again I was oblivious to the weather situation in the south! My current tracking book (little Woolworths note books that I used for recording everything I'd heard on my radio, and everything I saw), was coming to an end, so I decided to make the short walk into Stockport to get a new one. As I walked back from the town centre, I saw Trident 3 G-AWYZ (Shuttle 863 from Glasgow) and Laker Airways B.707 G-AVZZ (GK8614 from Detroit) both arrive in quick succession. I wasn't convinced they were diversions, but the next two arrivals dispelled all such doubts! British Airways B.747 G-AWNM at 0947 (BA889 from Bahrain) was quickly followed by British Caledonian DC-10 G-BEBL at 0950 (BR366 from Kano). A further flight, British Airways SVC-10 G-ASGI at 1000 (BA610 from Montreal) went overhead as I was putting my key in the door. For the next hour there was a steady flow of diversions, mainly mundane apart from Saudia B.747 OD-AGI at 1025 (SV071 from Rome), which was a new airline to Manchester. This particular aircraft, leased from MEA, was in full SV colours. Also during this session was the first visit of a Kenya Airways Boeing 707, with 5Y-BBI (KQ714 from Rome). When SVC-10 G-ASGD landed at 1114 (BA317 from Jeddah), it went very quiet for next two hours, despite the Heathrow RVR hovering around the 100m-200m mark. During this time numerous flights were turned away, possibly due to lack of staff and handling facilities. Included in these was Singapore Airlines B.747 9V-SQD which was heard later heading north towards Prestwick as 'Singapore 077'. My friend, Ian Barrie, had called in to see if I wanted to join the 'travelling posse' that was on its way to the airport. But once again I declined for the reasons mentioned previously. A decision that I would come to regret I might add! Aircraft started diverting into Manchester again from 1300, but as the runway had changed to runway 06, I wasn't going see anything now! A slight easterly breeze had picked up, which was obviously the reason for the runway change, and although there had been some patchy cloud in the morning, it had developed into a cold but sunny day. (Ian Barrie)

19th December 1977 – This afternoon shot shows two of the many first time visitors to Manchester today. Kenya B.707 5Y-BBI (KQ714 from Rome), which has been positioned onto the South Bay, is seen with Saudia B.747 OD-AGI (SV071 from Rome) basking in the winter sun. (Ian Barrie)

19th December 1977 – British Caledonian DC-10 G-BEBL & South African B.747 ZS-SAM 'Drakensburg' are seen with two of the hundreds of spotters that descended on the airport's terraces today. What a great way to start the Christmas holidays - with a nice diversion day! (MA Archive via Ringway Publications)

19th December 1977 – The next diversion session began with three first time visitors. El Al Boeing 707 4X-ATS at 1354 (LY315 from Tel Aviv), making the first appearance by the airline since November 1971; Boeing 747 G-BDXA at 1322 (BA510 from New York), the first visit of a British Airways Rolls-Royce powered B.747 and lastly, Malaysian Airlines DC-10 9M-MAS at 1359 (MH002 from Frankfurt). Both G-BDXA (stand 14) and Malaysian 9M-MAS (runway 28) can be seen in this shot. Other diversions during this period were Laker DC-10 G-AZZD at 1407 operating a Skytrain service (GK020 from New York); first time visitor Swissair DC-9-51 HB-IST at 1429 (SR816 from Geneva); KLM DC-8 PH-DEM at 1433 (KL119 from Amsterdam) and KLM DC-9 PH-DNB at 1439 (KL101 from Rotterdam). Again, this batch of diversions lasted for about an hour and more aircraft were turned away. Included in these was British Airways Concorde G-BOAD (BA301 Bahrain-Heathrow); British Airways B.747 G-BDXB (BA660 Miami-Heathrow); MEA B.707 OD-AFD (ME201 Beirut-Heathrow which diverted to Paris-Orly); Alia B.707 JY-ADP (RJ111 Amman-Heathrow) and finally British Airways L.1011 G-BBAH (BE003 Paris-Heathrow, diverted to Glasgow). Swissair DC-9-51 HB-ISM (SR804 Zurich-Heathrow) was actually inbound to Manchester, when it followed company instructions and diverted to Gatwick instead. British Airways Trident 2 G-AVFB (BE355 Rome-Heathrow) was also inbound to Manchester, but it eventually ended up diverting to Bournemouth. The diversions began again when British Airways BAC 1-11 G-AVMR arrived at 1655 (BZ705 from Aberdeen), followed forty-five minutes later by another Saudia flight this time one of their own aircraft, L.1011 HZ-AHD at 1739 (SV173 from Paris). Unfortunately, another Saudia L.1011, HZ-AHH, which was on delivery direct from the Lockheed factory routing Palmdale-Heathrow, was a possible diversion contender, but it went to Paris. There were no more diversions after 'Saudi 173', when there was a slight improvement in the RVR at Heathrow, enough to allow Cat.II and Cat.III aircraft to land. However, Cat.I aircraft were still having difficulties, resulting in the final Heathrow diversion of the evening, SVC-10 G-ASGF (BA717 from Doha) at 2123. During certain meteorological conditions, mainly anticyclones that were generating southerly winds, frequencies that could not be heard normally became audible. Sometimes they were faint, but other times they were quite strong. A good indicator of these conditions, was whether or not I could hear London Volmet North, a recorded weather information service covering three sectors, north/south/main. Volmet North (Volume Meteorogical) was broadcast on 128.6 and this evening and early the following morning were such occasions, when the frequency was audible. Disappointingly, the broadcast it gave for Heathrow at 0720 the following morning was Vis: 700m and improving, which indeed it did! I spent the 20th listening to the traffic departing back to Heathrow, in the hope there would be another high pressure bringing in lots of fog real soon! (Ian Barrie)

19ᵗʰ December 1977 – These two shots taken from late afternoon include El Al B.707 4X-ATS, British Airways SVC-10s G-ASGC (BA590 from Prestwick) & G-ASGL (BA383 from Tehran) and B.747 G-BDXA (BA510 from New York). (Both MA Archive via Ringway Publications)

20th December 1977 – DC-10 9M-MAS (MH002 from Frankfurt) became the only Malaysian Airlines DC-10 to visit Manchester. Their next appearance was eight years later, when B.747 9M-MHI diverted in on Sunday 6th January 1985. (Geoff Ball)

20th December 1977 – Saudia L.1011 Tristar HZ-AHD eventually departed for Heathrow this afternoon, as 'Saudi 1173'. The next Saudia diversion into Manchester would be November 1978 (B.747 OD-AGH). It would be four more years before another Tristar visit and on this occasion there would be two! (Geoff Ball)

20ᵗʰ December 1977 – Eastern England had also been affected by dense, freezing fog yesterday, so rather unusually, Air Anglia F.27 G-BDVT (AQ109 from Amsterdam) diverted into Manchester from Norwich. It is seen here parked next to Ford Air Gulfstream 1 G-ASXT. (Geoff Ball)

20ᵗʰ December 1977 – Kenya Airways B.707 5Y-BBI (KQ714 from Rome), was the first of the airline's three aircraft to make fairly regular diversionary visits until August 1983, when they purchased two Airbus A.310s. The first of these to visit Manchester was 5Y-BEN in October 1986. (Geoff Ball)

20th December 1977 – Air Anglia F.27 G-BCDO (AQ201 from Edinburgh) was the first of several morning diversions, arriving from places such as Leeds, Birmingham and East Midlands. The numerous diverted aircraft in the background would soon start to make a move, and return to Heathrow. (Andy Hall)

20th December 1977 – Saudia B.747 OD-AGI is attracting only mild interest from the spectators on pier B. It was one of three Boeing 747s leased from MEA from 1977-1981, until they took delivery of their own aircraft. (Geoff Ball)

18th January 1978 - Following a deterioration in Heathrow's weather in the early hours, Manchester apron control advised that should the need arise, eighteen narrow-bodied and four wide-bodied aircraft could be accepted. Heathrow was affected by dense, freezing fog all day, which restricted flights to just a handful of arrivals, but Gatwick was unaffected and took so many diversions that by 1500 arrivals were by PPO (prior permission only). Apart from the very first diversion into Manchester of B.747 VH-EBD at 0641 (QF001 from Bahrain) in a very low cloud base, little else of excitement appeared until the arrival of Alitalia DC-9 I-DIBC at 1122 (AZ282 from Rome), which heralded the start of a little more variety. Soon to follow was Austrian Airlines DC-9-51 OE-LDN at 1145 (OS451 from Vienna), Kenya Airways B.707 5Y-BBK at 1149 (KQ214 from Frankfurt) and Finnair DC-9-51 OH-LYR at 1156 (AY831 from Helsinki). British Airways B.747 G-AWNC arrived at 1204 (BA510 from New York), but there were no more diversions for three hours, so I assumed the Heathrow weather had improved. The walk home from school placed the flight path perfectly in front of us, but nothing appeared. Just as I got onto the balcony, about to enter my flat, I heard a loud rumbling that got louder and louder. I rushed as quickly as I could to the front window and saw British Airways L.1011 G-BBAF (BE079 from Nice), disappearing into the backdrop of the setting sun, on its final descent into Manchester. I later discovered that there had been no improvement in the Heathrow weather at all. In fact, during those 'three hours' I had missed two B747s. The first, TWA B.747 N93107 at 1501 (TW1754 from Shannon) which had originally diverted to Shannon, had attempted to return to Heathrow, before giving up and diverting into Manchester. I had every excuse for missing this because it sneaked in on runway 06. The second, Alia JY-AFA at 1547 (RJ111 from Amman) was one of the highlights of the year, a first visit for the airline and the aircraft, but I am still baffled as to how I'd missed it on my walk home! Soon to follow was Trident 3 G-AWZU at 1635 (BE195 from Barcelona) and El Al B.707 4X-ATB at 1638 (LY315A from Paris). There were further sporadic arrivals throughout the evening, culminating in another visit of a British Airways Concorde, G-BOAE this time, which arrived at 2047 (BA170 from New York). The Concorde flights to New York had been subjected to legal wrangling for many months, prior to their commencement on 22nd November 1977, initially operating twice a week. Although Manchester was still preparing to accept further diversions, with space being made for nine aircraft including three wide-bodied, no more arrived after the final diversion of the evening, Alitalia DC-9 I-DIZE at 2200 (AZ292 from Milan). The forecast predicted a vigorous low pressure, bringing wind and rain which would sweep across the country, so a weather standby was issued to expect strong winds. Finally, the following aircraft requested a diversion to Manchester but were refused, MEA Boeing 720 OD-AFS (ME201), Kuwait Airways B.707 9K-ACJ (KU183) and National Airlines DC-10 N83NA (NA002). (Shaun Connor)

18th January 1978 – This evening shot in the bitter cold captures EL AL B.707 4X-ATB, which last visited in December 1961; Ghana Airways VC-10 9G-ABO (GH700 from Accra) and British Airways L.1011 G-BBAF. (Geoff Ball)

18th January 1978 – Not a diversion, but weather related, was the final highlight of the day, Swissair Boeing 747 HB-IGB operating our own Zurich flight SR842/3. Due to fog at Heathrow, none of the airlines Zurich flights had operated, so they used Manchester's flight with its larger aircraft to bring their Heathrow-bound passengers to the UK and transport them onwards to Heathrow by surface transport.
(MA Archive via Ringway Publications)

19ᵗʰ January 1978 – Taken the following morning under grey and leaden skies, are two of yesterday's arrivals, Kenya Airways B.707 5Y-BBK & TWA B.747 N93107. (MA Archive via Ringway Publications)

3ʳᵈ May 1978 - Over 2,000 passengers arrived on various diverted flights due to fog at Heathrow and Gatwick. Space was made available for up to twenty aircraft, including five wide-bodied, but in the end nine wide-bodied were accepted. Seen here is British Caledonian B.707 G-CDHW (BR366 from Kano), two of the four British Airways B.747 arrivals, and Air India B.747 VT-EDU (A104 from New York). Unusually the New York flight operated by SVC-10 G-ASGA (BA184/5) is parked on gate 2. (Neil Lomax)

3rd May 1978 – There were a number of first time visitors today, starting with the very early morning diversion of Transmeridian Hong Kong CL-44 VR-HHC at 0443 (KK2733 from Lagos) on its only visit to Manchester. Previously registered as G-AWWB from 1968 to 1975, this aircraft operated for Transmeridian and later British Cargo until its sale in 1980. (Neil Lomax)

3rd May 1978 - A new airline to Manchester today was Delta Airlines, with the arrival of L.1011 Tristar N81028 at 0754 (DL010 from Atlanta). Having diverted from Gatwick, this was only the third day of operation of this new daily service to Atlanta. (Richard Corden).

3rd May 1978 – The visit of National Airlines Douglas DC-10 N81NA (NA002 from Miami) marked the final visit of the airline to Manchester. After several unsuccessful attempts at a takeover by a number of other US airlines, it was Pan Am that acquired a controlling majority in 1979, with the final acquisition taking place in January 1980. (John Harrington)

3rd May 1978 – British Airways B.747 G-AWNL (BA070 from Toronto) seen getting ready to return to Heathrow, was one of four during the morning. The other three were G-AWNB (BA006 from Anchorage), G-AWNC (BA270 from Boston) and first time visitor G-BDXC (BA012 from Bombay). Another B.747 first visit today was Qantas VH-EBN (QF001 from Bombay). (MA Archive via Ringway Publications)

13ᵗʰ October 1978 – British Caledonian DC-10 G-BEBL (BR362 from Lagos) was one of forty-two diversions. This figure was even more remarkable, because for around five hours from mid-morning to early afternoon, Manchester was also affected by fog which severely restricted its own flights, let alone diversions! A high pressure centred on the Azores had been bringing increasingly warm temperatures by the 9ᵗʰ October, which lasted for several days. Although the 12ᵗʰ was another warm day, the sunshine had been replaced by total cloud cover, but the weather forecast in the evening was predicting widespread and dense fog over much of the Midlands and southern England. The thought of what might happen the following morning, made it difficult to sleep and I woke up many times during the night to see if it was morning! I had taken my aircraft radio to bed with me, and each time I woke up I had a little scan across the frequencies, but there was little traffic around 2am. The morning finally arrived, but when I switched the radio on again there was no mention of bad weather. This 'disappointment' was short lived however, when I heard Gulfstream II N1806P talking to ground control about where he was parking, as he was "not familiar with Manchester". This sounded promising, but not yet proof there was fog around the country. I then heard 'Midland 210F' (Intra Airways DC-3 G-AMPO), a regular DC-3 freight flight into East Midlands, calling up on Manchester tower frequency, so it looked like we had a Luton and East Midlands diversion. Close behind on the ILS was British Airways B.707F G-ATWV (BA3670 from New York) on its final visit, but unfortunately it was on runway 06! All I could ever see in the way of aircraft from our flat was lights in the distance if the conditions were clear, but they weren't! It was very misty, and destined to get worse. Anyway, I quickly repositioned my radio from my bedroom back into the kitchen, where it was normally set up and it wasn't long before I heard 'Delta 010' working Manchester control frequency 125.1 declaring his intentions to divert to Manchester. He was confirming the landing runway would be 'runway 6', but by the time he had been transferred to Manchester approach, this was changed to runway 24! This was Delta's third diversion into Manchester (L.1011 N81028), so they were clearly happy with us. By the time Kenya Airways B.707 5Y-BBI arrived at 0805 (KQ414 from Rome), unbeknown to me, there had already been twenty-one diversions up to this point. These included JAT DC-9 YU-AHM at 0130 (JR2210 from Belgrade), Alaska International C-130 N107AK at 0219 (AK107 from Khartoum) and two British Airways Tristars, G-BEAL at 0229 (BE327 from Paris) & G-BEAM at 0538 (BA120 from Bombay). (Simon Lowe)

13ᵗʰ October 1978 – Another of those very early arrivals was a further Transmeridian Cargo CL-44, with G-AXAA (KK404 from Cairo). Although this flight was a Gatwick diversion, it is seen here making its way through the mist to the holding point of runway 24 and eventual departure for Stansted. The next diversion was Air India B.747 VT-EBN (AI108 from New York), which landed at 0828 after declaring an emergency about forty miles from touchdown, just as the fog at Manchester was closing in. Once on the ground, the aircraft was parked close to the fire station, where a full evacuation via the escape chutes took place. Forty-five firemen were involved with the incident, found to have been caused by an electronic organ in one of the cargo holds catching fire. It was the airport's first emergency evacuation of a Boeing 747. By the time the Air India had landed, no traffic was being accepted into Heathrow or Gatwick, unless they were Cat.III equipped. The weather situation at the London airports eased slightly around 1030, but even then landing was by prior permission only, which remained in force for most of the day. Being at school in Heaton Moor, and not knowing what was happening at the airport was extremely frustrating. The flight path was obscured by mist, so we could be missing seeing any diversions. However, we found out later that due to the dense fog affecting Manchester, the airport only received one diversion, which was Tradewinds CL-44 G-AWGS arriving at 1006 (IK4148B from Montreal). After this there were no more arrivals until 1333. Over the next few hours, the fog slowly began to lift, but it was still patchy enough to prevent any further diversions. Today's winner for diversions was definitely Prestwick. Amongst the endless trails heading northbound were Iraqi Airways B.747 YI-AGO (IA237), Braniff B.747 N601BN (BN602) & Malaysian DC-10 9M-MAS (MH002). By mid-afternoon, once the fog had lifted sufficiently, the airport made preparations based on the weather forecasts, with space being made available for up to twelve narrow-bodied aircraft, plus six wide-bodied. I stayed after school for half an hour longer than usual for an extra Maths lesson, and whilst walking home down Manchester Road towards Heaton Norris, things took a positive turn! In quick succession came two Heathrow diversions, British Airways Trident 3 G-AWZJ at 1643 (BE691 from Warsaw) and Trident G-AVFI at 1656 (BE601 from Vienna). Ironically at the same time these aircraft arrived, L.1011 G-BEAL left Manchester as 'Beeline 327X', attempting to return to Heathrow. The next three hours were fairly uneventful, but the anticipation of more diversions to Manchester was high, as the forecast for the southern airports was predicting a rapid deterioration from 1700 to 1900. By 2000 diversions were on their way from Heathrow and Gatwick. Although they were mostly mundane, a couple of interesting arrivals were Royal Air Maroc B.727 CN-CCG making the first visit of both aircraft and

airline at 2114 (AT5262 from Casablanca) and IAS DC-8F G-BDDE at 2122 (FF513A from Lagos). By 2030, Heathrow was below limits for most aircraft and Manchester ATIS was advising that due to visibility restrictions no traffic was being accepted for Gatwick. Meanwhile, the day had not been a good one for Air India, and was about to get worse! By 2050, their B.747 VT-EBN was ready to depart back to Heathrow, but during its takeoff run it burst a tyre, and remained on the runway for around half an hour. During this time, several inbounds had to overshoot and go into the hold over Manchester, but it managed to exit the runway before too long. I stayed up to hear one more diversion, Dan-Air Comet G-APMB at 2152 (DA2305 from Gerona), then took my radio to bed and had another brief listen. All seemed quiet, with not a lot to be heard. Unbeknown to me, Heathrow declared itself closed at 2330, which meant a further nine diversions, British Airways Tridents G-AVFB at 0020 (BE617 from Zurich), G-AWZF at 0023 (BE507 from Rome), G-AWZA at 0033 (BE4683 from Belfast), G-AWZP at 0037 (BE455 from Madrid), G-AWZJ at 0042 (BE737 from Hamburg) & G-AWZB at 0128 (BE619 from Zurich); Tristars G-BBAI at 2339 (BE387 from Brussels) & G-BBAE at 0118 (BE639 from Copenhagen) and first time visitor Alitalia B.727 I-DIRI at 2348 (AZ316 from Pisa). By the early hours after the last diversions had arrived, not only were disused runway 02/20 and runway 10/28 being used for the parking aircraft, taxiway 1 (at end of pier A to the holding point of runway 24) and taxiway 2 (from the end of B of the holding point of runway 06), were also pressed into use for parking. (Geoff Ball)

13th October 1978 – Eastern Airways DC-3 G-AMPO (BD210F from Amsterdam) as seen above, arrived bright and early on a British Midland freight flight as an East Midlands diversion. Today could have been one of the many occasions when Manchester would profit from a multitude of weather diversions, as Heathrow and Gatwick were fogged out for long periods. However, from mid-morning Ringway had weather problems of its own, which prevented many Heathrow-bound flights from diverting in. Even so, the airport still handled forty-two diversions of various sizes. (Geoff Ball)

14th October 1978 - As the morning weather steadily improved, the mass exodus of diverted aircraft back to Heathrow began. This caused major ATC problems, with considerable holding due the sheer number of flights returning, but the situation did not lead to any extra diversions. Seen in this early morning shot are three diversions from yesterday, British Airways L.1011 G-BEAM (BA120 from Bombay), Alitalia B.727 I-DIRI (AZ316 from Rome) & British Airtours B.707 G-ARWD (KT631 from Palma). (Geoff Ball)

14th October 1978 – Alitalia B.727 I-DIRI is seen passing the Tridents on the South Bay. In the background is IAS DC-8 G-BDDE, along with a British Airways Viscount and Trident in the distance. Three different Alitalia Boeing 727s diverting into Ringway between 1978 and 1981 (I-DIRI/DIRJ & DIRU) all made their first visits to Manchester during 1978. (Simon Lowe)

14th October 1978 – The hot and sunny weather of the previous few days was by now a distant memory! On a dull and misty afternoon, British Airways L.1011 G-BBAE (BE'AE) is seen on rotation off runway 24, departing back to Heathrow. (Simon Lowe)

14th October 1978 – As the Heathrow weather made much improvement, more aircraft made their way south, and despite holding delays inbound things were slowly returning to normal. Gatwick however was another story. Although their weather had been marginal during the morning, aircraft had carried on landing. Around lunchtime there was a brief deterioration, and I heard Braniff B.747 N601BN (BN602) in deep discussion with his operations at Gatwick, deciding if it was worth holding further, and hoping for an improvement in the RVR. About half an hour later whilst I was eating my lunch – two Spinks Cornish pasties to be exact, I was totally surprised and delighted when the same Braniff flight, B.747 N601BN (BN602 from Dallas) came screaming over the flats, touching down at 1242. Two more diversions following in quick succession were Dan-Air BAC 1-11s G-AWWX at 1247 (DA4027 from Hanover) & G-ATPL at 1255 (DA5568 from Berlin). One more Gatwick diversion was LOT TU-134 SP-LHF arriving at 1612 (LO4265 from Krakow). (Simon Lowe)

28th October 1978 – I had little sleep after hearing last night's weather forecast, predicting widespread fog in the south overnight. A couple of diversions just after midnight were Sudan Airways B.707 ST-AFB (SD128 from Rome) seen above on its first visit, and a much delayed Laker Airways flight, DC-10 G-AZZC (GK020 from New York) seen in the background. By the time I was up, a couple of British Caledonian flights which had already arrived were B.707 G-CDHW at 0641 (BR352 from Dakar) & DC-10 G-BEBM at 0653 (BR368 from Accra). (Simon Lowe)

28th October 1978 – After the two British Caledonian flights, soon to follow were British Airways L.1011 G-BBAJ at 0655 with a great sounding radio, and SVC-10 G-ASGH at 0722 (BA058 from Cairo). The next diversion to arrive, nearly two hours later was Air India B.747 VT-EDU at 0912 (AI110 from New York), making its third visit to Manchester. Although Heathrow and Gatwick were affected by fog right up until lunchtime, there were remarkably few diversions. Only ten arrived from 0640 to 1230, with most ending up at Bournemouth, Luton and Stansted. The majority of British Airways B.747 flights diverted to Prestwick. (Geoff Ball)

28th October 1978 – South African Airways B.747 ZS-SAP arriving at 1054 (SA228 from Johannesburg/Sal Island), was the last of the airlines five B.747-244Bs to make their first visits to Manchester. It was preceded by British Airways BAC 1-11 G-BBMF at 1002 (BA5631 from Inverness), which held for around forty minutes at Bovingdon, before venturing north again, into Ringway. (Geoff Ball)

28th October 1978 - DC-9-51 OH-LYO arriving at 1121 today (AY831 from Helsinki), was the first time that Finnair had used Manchester as a diversion alternate for their Heathrow flights. (Geoff Ball)

28th October 1978 – I heard the final diversions, British Caledonian B.707s G-AXRS at 1220 (BR246 from Houston) & G-BDLM at 1224 (BR676 from Caracas), talking to each other on their company frequency an hour before arrival. 'Caledonian 246' was holding over South Wales and 'Caledonian 676' from Caracas was holding in the Southampton area. Both were concerned they were low on fuel, and said "If they didn't make Gatwick at the first attempt, they were going to have problems". In the end they decided it was too much of a risk, and subsequently made the trip northwards! (Neil Lomax)

29th October 1978 - An early morning diversion witnessed by the writer, was first time visitor B.747 N93109 arriving at 0556 (TW760 from Los Angeles), still in the airline's old 'globe' colours. Heathrow was affected by fog until mid-morning and at 0720 their visibility was 0m with an RVR of 150m. As Ringway received just the one arrival, it appeared the weather diversions had gone elsewhere, even though Manchester could accept up to ten narrow-bodied and four wide-bodied aircraft. (Lloyd Robinson)

10th November 1978 – The weather forecast from the previous evening for the southeast was looking promising! Widespread fog was predicted, but the forecasts were notoriously hit-and-miss in terms of how intensive or dense it might be. When the BBC used the letters F-O-G on their weather report chart, the bigger the letters the more dense it would be, and the more spread out the letters, the more extensive it would be! In reality however, the opposite usually applied. When the letters were smaller, more chaos arose, and the letters were bigger nothing much seemed to happen! Not long after I had gone to bed before another school day, with the prospect of double English and double maths in the morning, the weather had read the script! Heathrow and Gatwick were below limits around 2200 and the diversions started to arrive soon afterwards. Five flights before midnight consisted of four from Gatwick and one from Heathrow, but the only one of interest was the first visit of Italian charter airline Itavia, who sent in DC-9 I-TIGI at 2300 (IH1538 from Genoa). The ATC watch log recorded that at this point, the airport would accept ten narrow-bodied and four wide-bodied diversions. This was the first of two visits by Itavia during 1978, with the latter being DC-9-15 I-TIGU on 22nd December 1978, which were both diversions. This Italian charter airline was a regular operator into Gatwick, serving various Italian cities until 1980, when this particular aircraft while en route from Bologna to Palermo, was 'officially' shot down on 27th June 1980. Although to this day the incident remains the subject to various other theories. However, all the speculation surrounding the airline led to a dramatic loss of confidence by the Italian travelling public. The airline was forced to suspend operations in December 1980, and they closed down permanently in July 1981. When the morning finally came, the weather forecast proved to be an accurate one. The very first diversion after midnight was Dan-Air Comet G-APMB at 0038 (DA2727 from Tenerife). Throughout the rest of the day, another forty-one diverted flights would arrive, as Gatwick was closed for most of the day due to the fog. I was up early around 0600, just in time to see and hear Saudia B.747 OD-AGH (SV077 from Riyadh), but another four British Airways flights which had already been in were L.1011 G-BEAL at 0230 (BA120X from Dhahran), SVC-10 G-ASGA at 0539 (BA130 from Jeddah), L.1011 G-BBAJ at 0551 (BA120 from Jeddah) & L.1011 G-BEAM at 0602 (BA100 from Bahrain). The local weather had not forecasted fog for the region, and for once they were right as it was a dull, nondescript day. It was hard to contain my excitement and anticipation of what was to come, as I settled down and listened in before leaving for school at 0820. (Dave Jones)

10ᵗʰ November 1978 - The next three diversions to arrive were British Airways B.747 G-BDXA at 0700 (BA012 from Bombay) seen here, British Caledonian B.707 G-AYEX at 0741 (BR214 from Lusaka) and Kenya Airways B.707 5Y-BBJ at 0810 (KQ416 from Rome). According to the ATC watch log, the number of diversions the airport was willing to accept had been revised just before G-BDXA arrived, to two narrow-bodied only. The next two diversions, G-AYEX and 5Y-BBJ, were in keeping with the revised quota, but B.747 G-BDXA seemed to dispel this! By 0820 the quota was revised again, this time to accept six narrow-bodied, but no wide-bodied diversions. By now, fifteen diversions had arrived since last night, including five wide-bodied. Before leaving for school I was listening to flight 'Delta 10' talking to his company. He was advised his alternate had been changed to Manchester, so what it was originally is a mystery! Reluctantly I left home and walked to school with my friend Ian Barrie. We discussed over and over how the day might develop, and hoped the fog would remain all day! We got as far as Heaton Chapel, with another ten minutes to go before we arrived at school, when we heard a distinctive aircraft noise. We turned around as the flight path was directly behind us, and saw it was a VC-10 with what looked like a dark tail. It was difficult to make out the airline as it was such a grey day, so we supposed it could only be British Airways or the RAF, as they were the only operators of VC-10s by now - or so we thought! When we got to school our friend told us it was actually Air Malawi (7Q-YKH), as he had heard it inbound on his radio. Ironically, I had my small Sharp portable radio with me, but it did not occur to me to switch it on. Delta L.1011 N81028 (DL010 from Atlanta) was next to follow, and we just about saw this from the classroom. There was nothing in the next hour, which always prompted the thought 'that's it then, the fogs cleared', but that was not the case. There were a couple more diversions, but we did not give them a second glance as they were two of Manchester's Heathrow flights (BA5001 & BA5003), which had failed to land at Heathrow. They were followed by Laker Airways Douglas DC-10 G-AZZD at 1020 (GK020 from New York). Another hour passed by before the next two arrivals, and we were pinned to the windows in the common-room during the morning break, desperate to see if anything was coming in. Our next lesson was Maths. Fortunately for us, this classroom commanded the best view of the flight path in the whole school block! I had my aircraft radio on in class, hidden under the desk, but it became a little too loud when 'Finnair 831' (DC-9-51 OH-LYR) called up on Manchester tower! Our maths teacher, Mr Swales, was not impressed and confiscated it until the end of the lesson! (Neil Lomax)

10th November 1978 - The first of today's many highlights from one of several extensive diversion sessions during the winter of 1978/79, was the only visit to Manchester by Air Malawi VC-10 7Q-YKH (QM142 from Nairobi/Blantyre) arriving at 0853. Ironically, the next diversion to land thirteen minutes later was Delta L.1011 N81028 (DL010 from Atlanta), which is visible in the background. (Dave Jones)

10th November 1978 - Ten minutes after the Finnair, Air France SE.210 F-BJTF was seen on the descent. Again, this did not get a second glance, but to us young spotters bunking off from school or for some of the older enthusiasts F-BJTF was interesting for three reasons. Firstly it was the first time since May 1973 that an Air France Heathrow flight had diverted into Manchester due to the weather. They would normally opt to return to Paris or divert to Gatwick, which was not possible as Gatwick had been closed all day due to

fog. Secondly, F-BJTF departed on a scheduled Heathrow-Toulouse flight (AF1823) once its passengers had arrived from London, with the return (AF1822) operating into Manchester. It arrived back at Manchester at 1805, along with another diverted Air France flight, Fokker F.28 F-GBBR (AF1862 from Nantes). Thirdly, F-BJTF would only make one more appearance at Manchester prior to its withdrawal on 21st March 1980. Also in shot is Laker Airways DC-10 G-AZZD, seen parked on the end of the domestic pier having recently arrived as a Gatwick diversion. Although the official line by lunchtime was that the airport could not accept any more diversions due to lack of space, it would accept Qantas B.747 VH-EBO (QF001), but it ultimately ended up at Prestwick along with fourteen other wide-bodied aircraft. Coming home from school for lunch was something I rarely did, but after consultation with my friend Ian, we decided to watch the BBC weather forecast on the lunchtime news. We were pleased when it predicted foggy weather for the rest of the day. As we walked back to school after lunch, in an almost repeat performance of the morning, we got to the same spot and heard an aircraft noise again, but this time it we identified it as British Caledonian DC-10 G-BEBL (BR366 from Kano), which was closely followed by IAS DC-8 G-BDDE (FF306 from Manston). The afternoon lesson was technical drawing, in a classroom where no aircraft could be seen. Fortunately for us nothing was missed due to a short-lived clearance in the London weather, when several aircraft made it back to Heathrow. Gatwick however was still suffering from dense fog that precluded any further arrivals for the rest of the all day. Once out of the classroom after the longest two hours imaginable, and into the fading light, the timing could not have been better! At that moment another British Caledonian aircraft appeared, in the form of Boeing 707 G-ATZC at 1605 (BR376 from Lagos). Once home, I took my aircraft radio into the comfort of the lounge to do some monitoring of the frequencies. I switched on the television, and Crackerjack had just started when the diversions started up again, and in greater numbers! The first of this batch were two Speedbird flights, Merchantman G-APEK at 1712 (BA3773 from Frankfurt) & Trident 3 G-AWZV at 1714 (BA691 from Warsaw). They were followed by Sabena B.737 OO-SDA at 1749 (SN611 from Brussels) and another Speedbird, B.747 G-AWNP (BA270), which had been making its way down from Prestwick to Heathrow when the RVR fell below its limits. By this time, Birmingham had stopped accepting diversions, although it too was affected by fog later in the evening. By 2030, East Midlands was no longer accepting diversions. Another eighteen diversions arriving throughout the evening brought the total to forty-two over the 24 hour period. Amongst these was the same Air France SE.210 that had been in earlier in the day, F-BJTF (AF1822 from Toulouse); Transavia B.737 PH-TVD in full British Airways colours (BA571 from Istanbul); a third Air France flight, Fokker F.28 F-GBBR (AF1862 from Nantes) and CTA SE.210 HB-ICN also operating a British Airways flight (BA615 from Zurich). The two highlights of the evening were yet to come! Around 2015 I heard on the radio what was clearly a B.747 identifying itself as '141', but I could not make out which airline it was. When he clarified, I kept missing what he said, so I monitored it the whole time it was on the approach frequency, but was still none the wiser! When it transferred to the tower I thought I would pick up the airline then, but I hadn't tuned in correctly, and I missed what he said again. I kept waiting in the hope I could identify it, so when it appeared its tail logo light made it easily identifiable as Kuwait Airways (B.747 9K-ADB). It was a fantastic sight and quite a surprise as I had no idea that they even had any Boeing 747s! The final highlight of the evening was the arrival of US Navy C-9 160049, diverting in from Upper Heyford, named 'City of Jacksonville'. Its full routing was Jacksonville-Andrews AFB-St. Johns, and it was carrying a number of admirals. It was lucky to land at Manchester, as by 2050 the airport had decided not to accept any further diversions, except for Concorde if requested. Twenty minutes later the airport agreed to accept C-9 160049 when 'Swing 78' arrived at 2141. Unlike the Kuwait B.747, I could easily identify the call-sign, although it meant very little to me! After staying up much later than I was used to (about 2230), I decided that was probably it for the night, as the frequencies had gone very quiet. Before bed I rang some of my friends to see if anyone was planning to go to the airport in the morning to see how many of the diversions were still in, and hopefully there would be some new ones as well. The conclusion to a very hectic and chaotic day was that British Airways and Servisair turned away many more aircraft, mainly because of handling problems caused by staff shortages, a situation that continued into the following day. Manchester wasn't the only airport suffering problems, as East Midlands took twenty-five diversions during the day and also turned away many more due to lack of space. Manchester airport called a management meeting later in the month, in an effort to improve organisation for any future large scale diversion days. (Dave Jones)

11ᵗʰ November 1978 – I caught the 8am No.369 bus to the airport, with several friends, and arrived forty-five minutes later to see if anything extra had sneaked in overnight. Before I left, it seemed that flights at Heathrow were still being affected by fog, which was still precluding landings for most aircraft. However due to the lack of parking space and handling equipment, Manchester would only accept four narrow-bodied and one wide-bodied diversion at this point. Seen here making a quick dash back to Gatwick, while the improvement in the weather lasted, is British Caledonian Douglas DC-10 G-BEBL. (Lloyd Robinson)

11ᵗʰ November 1978 - Not long after arriving at the airport and getting up onto the terraces, another British Airways B.747, G-AWNB (BA012 from Abu Dhabi), was taxiing in, adding to the already congested apron, bays, disused runway and even a normally active taxiway. Last night's star visitors, Kuwait Airways B.747 9K-ADB & US Navy C-9 160049 were still present. We could see 'Japan Air 423' holding over Pole Hill, but it eventually gave up on the fog lifting sufficiently enough to land, and diverted to Copenhagen. It wasn't long before aircraft started to make a move back to Heathrow, such as British Airways/Transavia Boeing 737 PH-TVD seen above. (Simon Lowe)

11th November 1978 – Today's star visitor was Western B.720 N93145 (WA9040 from Bangor), diverting in from Stansted, which was eventually destined to become HZ-NAA. (Geoff Ball)

11th November 1978 – Another morning shot shows US Navy C-9A 160049 parked on the domestic pier, having diverted in the previous evening as 'Swing 78'. There are still plenty of aircraft in the background, including the C-9A with its thrust reversers still open. In 2011, 160049 was finally retired from the US Navy after twenty-five years of service. (Simon Lowe)

11th November 1978 - Kuwait Airways operated four Boeing 747-200s from 1978-1995, which all visited Manchester at various times. Seen parked on stand 24, is 9K-ADB, which would shortly return to Heathrow. (Lloyd Robinson)

11th November 1978 – Although British Airways Viscount G-AOYI was operating a Ronaldsway-Manchester flight and was not a diversion, this shot captures the extent of the diversions littering the various parking areas. (Geoff Ball)

11ᵗʰ November 1978 – Air Malawi VC-10 7Q-YKH is seen mid-morning returning to Gatwick. In the early 1970s the African-airline had been looking for an aircraft to operate its International services, and in 1974 they purchased VC-10 G-ASIW from British Caledonian. Re-registered as 7Q-YKH, it operated their London services into Gatwick, and served the airline for five years until its withdrawal and storage at Bournemouth in late-1979. By this time, Air Malawi was the only airline apart from British Airways still operating the type on international services. In 1981 it was reactivated and flown to Blantyre, but only for a further period of storage before being broken up in 1995. (Simon Lowe)

11ᵗʰ November 1978 – IAS Douglas DC-8F G-BDDE (FF306 from Manston) was making the last of its three visits to Ringway. On 15ᵗʰ August 1979, IAS merged with Transmeridian to form British Cargo Airlines, comprising of a fleet of fifteen aircraft, but the new airline folded seven months later. The probably reasons for the collapse were the recession and the increasingly high cost of fuel. (Neil Lomax)

11th November 1978 – Although RAF VC-10 XR806 (RR2298 from Nairobi) arrived on diversion just before midday, aircraft were starting to disperse from the aprons, departing to where they were meant to be! Boeing 720 N93145 was part of this exodus, and is seen taxiing to the holding point for departure off runway 24. (Simon Lowe)

11th November 1978 – This rather poor quality shot of British Airways Trident 3 (BE'ZV) returning to Heathrow, further emphasises how far behind the airline was in repainting its aircraft into the new colours, particularly their Trident fleet! (Paul Deakin)

11th November 1978 – Laker Airways Boeing 707 G-BFBS seen above is a yet another aircraft departing for Gatwick. As of 1240, Heathrow had a visibility of 1200m and Gatwick 2000m. By now my friends and I had left the spectator terraces and were camped out at the landing lights, by the crossroads between Ringway Road and Shadow Moss Road. A few Luton diversions arrived during the afternoon, which included Trans Europa SE.210 EC-BRX (TR248 from Palma) and Falcon 10 HB-VDX. Below, Kenya Airways B.707 5Y-BBI is seen passing Pelican Cargo B.707F G-BEVN sat on the South Bay. The Pelican aircraft had been moved four times since its arrival on the 9th November. Twice on the South Bay, then to gate 46 and runway 28, presumably to accommodate all the diversions! (Both Simon Lowe)

11th November 1978 – Kuwait Airways B.747 9K-ADB seen above in the gathering gloom, was also returning to Heathrow. The Manchester weather became increasingly worse as the day progressed. Although there seemed to be a moderate breeze, it became very cold, with swirling fog. (Simon Lowe)

11th November 1978 - From 1500 to 1600, the weather had deteriorated rapidly. Whilst waiting for the bus home, British Midland Viscount G-AZLT (BD932 from Ronaldsway) arrived at 1611 as a Liverpool diversion. By the time I got back, I wasn't expecting any more diversions, as the forecast predicted early evening fog. I decided to watch TV, oblivious to the fact that visibility at Gatwick had dropped yet again. I missed two Gatwick diversions, Wardair DC-10 C-GXRB as 'Wardair 410' and Balair DC-9 HB-IDT (BB182 from Zurich) which were both first time visitors to Manchester. (Simon Lowe)

5th December 1978 – The previous day and weekend had seen some atrocious weather, ranging from a very wet Saturday to a cold, dull and windy Sunday, which transformed to calmer conditions resulting in patchy fog during the morning of the 4th. This morning's diversions included first time visitor British Airways B.747 G-BDXB at 0923 (BA270 from Boston) and an infrequent visit by TWA, with the arrival of B.747 N93119 at 1002 (TW770 from Detroit). Manchester's weather deteriorated around 1030, about the same time the fog in the southeast was starting to thin. By early evening, Blackpool and Warton were affected, and a couple of British Island Airways Heralds from Ronaldsway arriving as Blackpool diversions were G-ASBG at 1844 (UK512) and G-APWF at 1847 (UK708). The ultra-rare HS.125, G-AVRF, which was only ever seen at Warton, also arrived at 1822. I spent the rest of the evening waiting for the inevitable, for the south to be affected by fog, as promised by the weather forecasters. The first to arrive was British Airways SVC-10 G-ASGI at 2152 (BA178 from New York), followed by British Airtours B.707 G-APFL at 2333 (BA583 from Larnaca). I took my aircraft radio to bed with me that evening, but found it difficult to sleep due to the anticipation of the following day. A short time later I heard a very loud and prolonged roar. Half asleep, I jumped out of bed and as I looked through my bedroom window I saw a familiar shape on approach. My heart leapt, as it was Concorde! I rushed to the front of the flat and from the kitchen window I watched it pass over into the distance on its descent. I went back to my bedroom and switched the radio on just in time to hear 'Speedbird Concorde 172 clear right on the greens'. I did not know what time it was, but I found out later it was not long before 0200! The fog was still affecting Heathrow by early morning and L.1011 G-BEAL (BA100 from Bahrain) arrived as I woke up. I heard it on the radio, talking to its company at Manchester. After this, Qantas B.747 VH-EBK (QF001 from Bahrain), made its first visit, arriving at 0651, which sounded really good over the radio. Two more diversions arriving from Heathrow before I left for school were B.747 G-AWNF at 0838 (BA062 from Nairobi) and Merchantman G-APEK at 0842 (BE3773 from Frankfurt). The ATC watch log recorded that at 0805, the airport was in a position to receive ten narrow-bodied diversions, but only two wide-bodied aircraft. The morning was very disappointing however, with only a small number of Leeds and Birmingham diversions received. I perked up though when Air New Zealand DC-10 ZK-NZS (BA282 from Los Angeles) as seen above, arrived on runway 06 at 1222. This was the airline's first visit to Manchester since December 1975, due to Prestwick being firmly established as their diversion alternate. (John Harrington)

5th December 1978 – The morning was rather lean for Heathrow diversions, despite the RVR remaining below limits for landing aircraft, but from late morning to early afternoon they started to arrive. Apart from the Air New Zealand DC-10, the others were Icelandair B.727 TF-FIE seen above (FI450 from Keflavik), British Airways B.707 G-ATZD (BA264 from Kingston), British Airways Merchantman G-APEG (BA3753 from Copenhagen), Air India B.747 VT-EBO (AI102 from New York) & Kenya Airways B.707 5Y-BBJ (KQ114 from Zurich). Also worth a mention was Qantas B.747 VH-EBK, which returned to Manchester around lunchtime, nearly three hours after it departed and attempted to land at Heathrow. Below is recently arrived British Airways B.747 G-BDXF. From around 1400, the Heathrow weather improved slightly enough for aircraft to start landing again, subject to ATC flow control. The number of Heathrow diversions could have been much higher, had Gatwick been affected and not taken so many diversions, including two Iran Air Boeing 747SPs, EP-IAA (IR777 from Tehran) & EP-IAC (IR776 from New York). Today also saw the first visit this year of a Douglas DC-6 other than OH-KDA, when Balair's sole example, HB-IBS (BB774 from Balair), diverted in at 1330 due to fog at Birmingham. (Both Hubert Parrish)

5th December 1978 – Two shots of the recently arrived Air India B.747, VT-EBO (AI102 from New York), which became the latest of the airline's B.747s to appear at Manchester. It would make two further visits, before being damaged beyond repair in a landing accident at Delhi in May 1990. (Both Hubert Parrish)

5th December 1978 – Balair DC-9 HB-IDT (BB776 from Zurich) arrived as a Birmingham diversion, along with DC-6 HB-IBS (BB774 from Zurich). Dense all day fog in the Midlands resulted in both Birmingham and Coventry being closed all day. (Hubert Parrish)

5th December 1978 – Kenya Airways B.707 5Y-BBJ (KQ114 from Zurich) is seen making its second visit to Manchester. (Hubert Parrish)

5th December 1978 – This mid-afternoon shot includes Concorde G-BOAD and Icelandair B.727 TF-FIE. Note the number of spectators (or lack of), at the end of pier B, a far cry from chaos of the first Concorde visit in November 1976. To be fair though, it was another school and working day, and Concorde continued to be a crowd puller right up until the last aircraft flew in 2003. (Hubert Parrish)

5th December 1978 – Another shot taken from the domestic pier, shows Balair DC-9 HB-IDT flanked by two British Airways Super 1-11s. Seen in the background are B.747s G-BDXF & VT-EBO and B.707 5Y-BBI. (Hubert Parrish)

5th December 1978 - The early morning arrival of Concorde G-BOAD did not appear to be any different from the others in the fleet. Even though it was dark, from my home I could still make out its British Airway's scheme on the starboard side, but unbeknown to me the port side was in full Singapore Airlines colours! British Airways had commenced operations to Singapore in December 1976, but were suspended after only a few weeks following the Malaysian government's refusal to allow flights over their airspace. The dispute had been finally settled in October 1978, and flights started up again the following month, hence the Singapore Airlines colours. (Hubert Parrish)

5th December 1978 – An impressive South Bay line-up consisting of a Lear Jet, Douglas DC-9, two C-130s and a Douglas DC-6! This day will be remembered for the airport receiving sixty-six diversions, from twelve different airports, the highest number handled by Manchester in a single day! The airport was deluged with diversions, particularly commuter aircraft, from late afternoon to early evening. Weather wise, the low pressure that had already arrived at Manchester, would sweep eastwards and bring with it the usual wind and rain. The United Kingdom was about to be a hit by the worst winter since 1963! (Hubert Parrish)

22nd December 1978 – In this late evening shot, Swissair DC-9-51 HB-ISK, Olympic B.707 SX-DBE and Itavia DC-9 I-TIGU, are just three of today's diversions, along with our own Air Malta B.720 9H-AAK operating KM700/1. As if the diversion session on the 5th was not enough for one month, today produced a further forty-eight diversions, and unlike the arrivals on that day, virtually all were airliners. By 0920 Heathrow was only accepting Cat.III aircraft due to fog, but the fog affecting Gatwick earlier on had lifted sufficiently enough for it to accept arrivals, including some diversions from Heathrow. Having got out of bed just when it was getting light, and realising it was another grey day just like yesterday, I went back to bed and decided to listen to the radio. I liked our local radio station, Piccadilly 261, and also enjoyed Simon Bates and his Golden Hour feature on Radio One, but when I heard a travel report around 1030 mentioning how bad the weather was in the south, I decided to get up and investigate. It did not take long before I realised that Heathrow in particular was having problems. Although Cat.III aircraft only were being accepted at Heathrow and Gatwick, the first diversion of the morning did not arrive until 1127, when World Airways DC-10 N104WA (WO104 from New York) became the catalyst to the opening of today's floodgates! Some of the diversions that followed included first time visitor Transavia B.737 PH-TVI at 1239 (EI154 from Dublin), KLM DC-9 PH-DNH at 1333 (KL125 from Amsterdam) and three British Airways Tridents, G-AVFF (BA375 from Brussels), G-AVYC (BA757A from Munich) & G-AVYE (BA805 from Dublin); and the first of two Gulf Air L.1011s during the day, with first time visitor N41020 arriving at 1421 (GF007 from Abu Dhabi). After this, Heathrow and Gatwick had a temporary improvement in the fog for about two hours, during which time a limited amount of movements were possible, although these were strictly controlled by ATC restrictions. However, this was short lived, as by 1600 both Heathrow and Gatwick were only accepting Cat.III traffic again. By 1720, Gatwick was closed for the rest of the day due to the weather and the congestion from handling a number of Heathrow diversions. The first flight to start the late afternoon/early evening rush of diversions was British Airways SVC-10 G-ASGL at 1554 (BA150 from Cairo). The number of diversions received in the next three hours was staggering! From 1715 to 1939 there were thirty-eight arrivals, twenty-six of which were diversions. Both Arrival frequency (119.4) manned by ATCO Gerry Stevens and Director (121.35) manned by Tony Brown, were in use for most of the evening. Both controllers were extremely efficient and professional. Amongst the highlights of this batch were Sobelair B.737 OO-SBQ at 1717, the first visit of another Alitalia B.727 with I-DIRJ at 1722 (AZ290 from Milan), Lufthansa B.727s D-ABKH at 1806 (LH052 from Dusseldorf) & D-ABHI at 1928 (LH070 from

Munich) and B.737 D-ABHE at 1913 (LH052 from Hamburg). Another Gulf Air L.1011 first time visitor was A4O-TW at 1811 (GF025 from Bahrain). Other arrivals included first time visitor Itavia DC-9 I-TIGU at 1828 (IH1540 from Rome); Boeing 707 SX-DBE at 1837 (OA259 from Athens) making the first visit of Olympic Airways since 1976; Swissair DC-9-51s HB-IST at 1848 (SR806 from Zurich) & HB-ISK at 1920 (SR812 from Geneva); Dan-Air Comets G-APMB at 1852 (DA3269 from Munich) & G-BDIT at 1904 (DA3215 from Hamburg); two British Airways Merchantman, G-APEJ at 1925 (BA3765 from Geneva) & G-APET at 1931 (BA3795 from Alicante) and KLM DC-8 PH-DEL at 1933 (KL137 from Amsterdam). Finally Eastern Airways L.1011 N323EA, arriving at 1922 (BA453 from Madrid) and on lease to British Airways, had a heated argument with British Airways Operations at Manchester, when they told him Ringway could no longer accept him. He was none too happy to say the least! He said "He really didn't have many other options", and stated in no uncertain terms "He would be diverting into Manchester anyway!" BA Ops were in absolute chaos, with the frequency in constant use the whole time. I recorded the poor lady manning the frequency saying to 'Speedbird 623' (L.1011 G-BBAE BA623 from Geneva), "We are up the wall here!" At around 1915, a union representative voiced his concerns over the number of diversions the airport was dealing with. It was stretching the various handling agents to their limits, but he was told that a number of aircraft still up in the air had no alternative other than to divert into Manchester. By the time British Caledonian BAC 1-11 G-AWYV arrived at 1939 (BR404 from Geneva), the airport was refusing anymore until further notice, unless it was an emergency. All available space was taken up by diverted aircraft, including the disused runway and runway 28. Lufthansa B.727 D-ABHI which was parked on domestic stand 48 reported at 2203, "That its passengers had been waiting for more than two hours to disembark, and were causing trouble by threatening to walk off the aircraft". At 2215 several people were observed leaving the aircraft without permission, and when it was towed to international stand 3 ten minutes later, it was minus twelve passengers! (Peter Hampson)

23rd December 1978 – The day started cheerfully enough, but the weather went rapidly downhill! By the afternoon, wind and rain was sweeping through the region, clearing away any remnants of the recent foggy weather. Gulf Air Tristar A4O-TW seen above parked on gate 26, has plenty of activity going on around it, whilst the other Gulf Air Tristar, N41020 leased from TWA, is out of shot but parked on gate 24. (Richard Corden)

23rd December 1978 - The morning after the night before! Although Heathrow was affected by dense fog until mid-morning, it came as no surprise that Manchester did not accept any more diversions! Boeing 707 SX-DBE is about to depart for Heathrow (OA260), and it would be further eight years before another Olympic Airways aircraft would visit Ringway again. (Barry Swann)

23rd December 1978 - L.1011 G-BBAE, was one of two British Airways Tristars diverting in last night, with the other being N323EA (BA453). British Airways Viscount G-AOYS has recently arrived from Ronaldsway (BA5571) and in the background parked on runway 28 is British Caledonian B.707 G-AYEX (BR334). (Richard Corden)

23rd December 1978 – Tradewinds CL-44 G-AWDK (IK5080) is seen the morning after, parked on the ex-Fairey apron. This demonstrates how much the airport was running out of space, as this part of the airfield was seldom used for the parking of diversions. Since the demise of Faireys in late-1977, the hangar itself had been used for storing pre-fabricated bridge sections for export. (Simon Lowe)

23rd December 1978 – The police Mini and the Dakota indicate that this photograph could have been easily taken in the 1960s! Skyways Douglas DC-3 G-AMSV (SM985 from Belfast) had arrived yesterday at 1451 as a Birmingham diversion, and seen in the background is the newly erected Air Kilroe hangar, with a sole PA-23 Aztec parked outside. (Richard Corden)

23ʳᵈ December 1978 – Comet G-BDIT (DA3215) seen parked in the South Bay, is making its final visit to Manchester. From March 1979, the airline would no longer have any Comets based at Ringway, although the occasional aircraft would still visit. By the end of October 1980, all their remaining Comets had been withdrawn. (Richard Corden)

31ˢᵗ December 1978 – A deep depression moving eastwards across the south on the 29ᵗʰ, was preceded by a cold air system, bringing snow to all areas. Late on the 30ᵗʰ, severe gales made the measurement of snow impossible in the southwest, but drifts were estimated to be 6ft high. The southeast was affected late evening, when diversions started to arrive, initially from Gatwick. First time visitor Qantas B.747 VH-EBM (QF001 from Bahrain) was one of several Heathrow diversions the following morning. (Simon Lowe)

31ˢᵗ December 1978 - Today's diversions were due to heavy snow in the southeast, affecting Heathrow and Gatwick. The first arrivals prior to midnight were Dan-Air B.707 G-AYSL (DA1033 from Palma), British Caledonian G-BCAL (BR554 from Tripoli) & G-CDHW (BR682 from Las Palmas). By 0700, Manchester had space for nine narrow-bodied and two wide-bodied diversions. This was amended frequently during the morning and early-afternoon. Liverpool Airport stated that although refuelling was unavailable, they could accept up to forty-five diversions! A further fifteen arrived before Gatwick and Heathrow re-opened around 1500, but with ATC restrictions. Apart from the new Qantas, other highlights were first visits by TMA B.707F OD-AGO at 0940 (TL171 from Beirut) & BWIA B.707 9Y-TEZ at 0953 (BW900 from Bridgetown). Delta Airlines diverted their Atlanta flight into Ringway again, this time with L.1011 N31029 (DL010). Both shots show its arrival on runway 06 at 1141. (Above Simon Lowe, below Barry Swann)

31ˢᵗ December 1978 – Although TMA B.707F OD-AGO (TL171) was a first time visitor, its arrival did not raise many eyebrows as the airline had been making regular visits of late, operating a number of flights to Beirut as an extension of their Monday Heathrow service (last one operated 11ᵗʰ December). As seen in this shot and others of the day, Manchester had its share of snow, but nothing like the amount in other areas. Nevertheless, there was a cold and biting easterly wind, which intensified after sunset. (Simon Lowe)

13ᵗʰ January 1979 - New Years Day had started brightly enough, but it soon clouded over, and by early afternoon it was thick enough for snow. Sure enough it snowed, on and off until the following morning, which was another cold and grey day with more snow. It was the beginning of a difficult and problematic month for many reasons. By the 3ʳᵈ January it was back to school, but the following day it was announced that it would have to close, for several weeks due to the lack of heating oil and burst water pipes! The rest of the month was dominated by strikes, with the winter of 1978/79 becoming known as the 'winter of discontent', as the period saw the biggest stoppage of labour since the 1926 general strike. Everyone seemed to be on strike, including ambulance drivers, lorry drivers, grave diggers, bin-men, car workers and so on. The airport was affected when firemen took action during the last week of January. Customs officers also went on strike on a number of occasions, but their action had less of an impact. The strikes and wintry weather all added to the country's problems, making January a thoroughly difficult and miserable month! However, the blockades of the country's docks by lorry drivers and the bad weather restricting road and shipping movements, gave Manchester a great variety of freight flights. Meanwhile the airport was getting negative comments due to the continuing problems with the 24 & 06 glidepath. There was also negative feedback from various airline captains. They complained that the airport had failed to address the lack of availability of all landing aids, especially during the current weather conditions. On the 11th January, two days before the above photograph was taken, the airport was hit with a considerable amount of snowfall and then fog, which reduced the speed on the regions motorways to 50mph. There were only nine arrivals at Manchester all day, but not specifically due to the weather. Overnight on the 12th/13th, the airport was hit by record low temperatures, when -12°C was recorded, making it the coldest January since 1945. Even the de-icing equipment was affected, when a number of vehicles were frozen solid. The airport struggled to operate normally until mid-afternoon, when it was subjected to patchy and occasionally dense freezing fog. In between the patchy fog, two British Midland diversions managing to arrive from Liverpool were DC-9 OH-LYB (BD386 from Heathrow) & Viscount G-AZNB (BD992 from Belfast). (Richard Corden)

19th January 1979 – The airport was affected by strong winds, cold temperatures and snow showers throughout the day. Due to weather conditions in the south, restrictions were imposed for traffic landing at Heathrow and Gatwick during the morning. While both airports were closed from 1230-1400 for snow clearance, Manchester received four diversions in a thirty minute period. They were Air New Zealand DC-10 ZK-NZQ at 1236 (BA598 from Los Angeles), Aer Lingus B.737 EI-ASG at 1253 (EI158 from Dublin), Bangladesh Biman B.707 S2-ABN at 1300 (BG003 from Dubai) as seen above, British Airways BAC 1-11 G-AVML at 1305 (BA743 from Cologne) and first time visitor Transmeridian DC-8F G-BFHW at 1411 (KK7675 from Las Palmas). The ATC watch log recorded that Manchester was preparing to accept up to twenty narrow-bodied and five wide-bodied aircraft, but in the end fifteen diversions were received from various airports. (Geoff Ball)

21ˢᵗ January 1979 – Today was a case of 'what might have been'. This January morning started promising enough with early diversions, which included British Caledonian B.707 G-BDLM arriving at 0532 (BR322 from Banjul) & DC-10 G-BEBM at 0556 (BR362 from Lagos) and Zambia Airways B.707 9J-ADY at 0641 (QZ038 from Lusaka). Gatwick and Heathrow were being affected by patchy fog, but as the visibility was constantly fluctuating, most aircraft managed to land normally. These were followed by Gatwick diversions Britannia Airways G-AVRM arriving at 0749 (BY459B from Athens) and Transvalair CL-44 HB-IEN at 1011 (VX121 from Kano). Stansted diversion DC-8F G-BTAC which arrived at 0907 (KK7677 from Las Palmas) is pictured above, and Falcon 20 OY-AZT at 1011 from Billund arrived as an East Midlands diversion. The Transvalair landed at a time when Manchester's weather was deteriorating rapidly, and by 1030 the fog was so bad it prevented any further arrivals until nine hours later. Simultaneously, Heathrow suffered the same fate, when it too fell below limits for most aircraft. A mad scramble for somewhere to land soon took place by the holding aircraft that were getting low on fuel. Gatwick, Heathrow, Stansted and Luton were then fogbound until around teatime. By 1100 the sight of four British Airways B.747s in close proximity to each other, were amongst many other diversions seen heading towards Prestwick under a clear blue sky. Although frustrating, it was also a very impressive sight! They were interspersed with other aircraft heading north, such as Air Canada B.747 C-FTOE, Braathens B.737 LN-SUM and two TWA flights, L.1011 N31031 (TW754) & B.747 N93106 (TW760). The situation became desperate when even Cardiff received a number of diversions and Aer Lingus Dublin-London flights were flight planned straight into Cardiff for a time. Other rarely heard flights diverting as far north as Prestwick, included Monarch Airlines B.720 G-BCBB (CY326 Larnaca-Heathrow) and B.707 4X-ATR (LY1315 Tel Aviv-Heathrow). Normality returned early evening, but as far as Manchester was concerned it went from the sublime to the ridiculous, when just as the fog was starting to clear; Ringway was hit by a 24 hour strike, forcing the cancellation of all scheduled flights from Manchester. Ten thousand passengers were affected, when porters, baggage handlers, car parking staff and firemen joined a nationwide stoppage. (Geoff Ball)

7th February 1979 – The UK's airports were suffering from snow and ice again today. Although Manchester had weather problems of its own, particularly with ice, it was put on possible standby for snow diversions from Heathrow, and could handle up to twenty narrow-bodied and four wide-bodied aircraft. Of the nine diversions arriving from 0947-1238, five were from British Airways. Others were Kenya Airways B.707 5Y-BBJ at 0947 (KQ214 from Frankfurt), SAS DC-9 SE-DAL at 1118 (SK501 from Copenhagen), first time visitor Alitalia DC-9 I-DIZO at 1138 (AZ282 from Rome) & SAS DC-9 OY-KGK at 1238 (SK515 from Stavanger). The trend of snow, frost, fog, ice and strong winds at Manchester over the next few days, continued until end of the month. (Geoff Ball)

18th February 1979 - A surprise diversion from the previous evening was Cessna 441 5Y-NCA, routing from Keflavik-Luton on delivery to Nairobi. It arrived with major engine trouble and was eventually moved to the Air Kilroe hangar for repair, before finally departing on the 2nd March for Heraklion. (Geoff Ball)

24th February 1979 - The first Caribou to visit Manchester was former Kuwait Air Force example C-GVYZ, seen here on the South Bay. It arrived at 1955 on the 22nd, having developed an engine fault whilst on delivery from Cherbourg to its new owner in Quebec. It finally departed on the 4th March. (Richard Corden)

17th March 1979 - Bad weather affecting the UK since New Year's Day continued to cause problems. Although Manchester had been affected by snow which restricted operations yet again, the airport was still able to accept Teesside diversion British Air Ferries Herald G-BEYD, arriving at 1109 from Rotterdam. This aircraft served British Air Ferries (later British Island Airways), until 1982 when it was withdrawn. Two years later it was broken up. (Geoff Ball)

3rd June 1979 - In the middle of a hot spell, there was surprising number of early/mid-morning fog diversions from Stansted, Luton and Birmingham. Included in these eight diversions was Maersk Air B.720 OY-APY arriving at 1056 (DM225 from Stockholm). (Barry Swann)

3rd June 1979 – Tarom Tupolev TU-154 YR-TPC (RO767 from Constanta) arriving as a Birmingham diversion, had already made its first visit to Manchester four days earlier. One of eleven different Tarom TU-154s to visit from 1976-1995, the last was made by YR-TPF on 23rd September 1995. (Paul Deakin)

3rd June 1979 - SE-DGK (LF063 from Stockholm), was one of two Linjeflyg Fokker F.28s diverting in this morning from Stansted. These were the only Linjeflyg aircraft to visit Manchester in their own colours. During the 1990s, the airline was absorbed into SAS and occasionally visited in their colours. (Barry Swann)

10th August 1979 - Citation 550 G-BFLY arrived at 1232 today from Reykjavik, on delivery to Northair Aviation, Leeds. It attempted to depart for Nice the following day, but returned with a technical problem, before leaving an hour later. It returned again on the 21st and remained inside the South Side hangars until its departure on the 25th. It was sold later in the year as HB-VGR. (Geoff Ball)

5th September 1979 – Whilst having my lunch at home, I witnessed the arrival of a very smart Douglas DC-3, HZ-TA3, making its descent into Manchester at 1345, routing from Houston to Riyadh on its delivery flight. This aircraft, with its full VIP interior, dropped in due to a shortage of the appropriate fuel at Prestwick. Operated by a Saudi prince until 1984, it was heard to be still flying in New Zealand in late-2012 as ZS-MRU. (Both Richard Corden)

11th October 1979 – A weak ridge of high pressure hanging on in the southeast of the UK produced the first crop of autumn diversions. The day saw ten wide-bodied aircraft on the ground at the same time, which was equal to the previous record set on 16th December 1975. Amongst them were three first time visitors, Lufthansa Airbus A300 D-AIAA at 0951 (LH050 from Dusseldorf); Pan American B.747 N751PA at 1036 (PA106 from Washington) making the US airline's first diversion to Manchester since August 1976; and finally Air New Zealand DC-10 ZK-NZM at 0931 (BA074 from Montreal). Others included Air India B.747 VT-EDU at 1001 (AI106 from New York) and British Airways B.747s G-AWND (BA012 from Dubai) & G-AWNE (BA190 from Washington). Finally, LOT Il-62 SP-LAC arriving at 0801 (LO4789 from Warsaw), had to park across two stands as the airport had no tow-bar for it! (Mark White)

11th October 1979 – This view from the ATC tower building, shows Air New Zealand DC-10 ZK-NZM, Lufthansa A300 D-AIAA, British Airways B.747 G-AWND and stored B.707 N473RN, a permanent fixture on the South Bay from August 1979 to February 1980. (MA Archive via Ringway Publications)

11ᵗʰ October 1979 – Another view from the tower looking towards the northwest shows B.747s N751PA & VT-EDU, along with British Airways VC-10s G-ASGC (stand 25) & G-ASGL (stand 26). G-ASGC had arrived on our flight as BA184 (from New York/Prestwick) and would eventually position to Heathrow once their weather situation had improved. This was also its final visit before withdrawal later in the month. In April 1980, it was flown to Cosford for preservation. Finally, G-ASGL had positioned from Heathrow to operate the outbound Prestwick/New York service (BA185). (MA Archive via Ringway Publications)

15ᵗʰ October 1979 – The airport was on early morning standby for possible London weather diversions, and could accept up to eight narrow-bodied and eight wide-bodied aircraft, but the first arrival was Hawarden diversion HS.125 HB-VGG at 0837 from Stuttgart. It was followed by British Caledonian DC-10 G-BGAT at 0840 (BR246 from Houston), the first of eight wide-bodied diversions in an hour. The others were Delta L.1011 Tristar N81028 at 0855 (DL010 from Atlanta) seen above, British Airways B.747 G-

AWNH at 0905 (BA260 from Bermuda), South African Airways B.747 ZS-SAO at 0908 (SA234 from Abidjan), Air India B.747 VT-EBO at 0915 (AI116 from New York), British Airways B.747 G-BDPV at 0918 (BA020 from Dubai), British Airways B.747 G-AWNI at 0923 (BA278 from Miami) and TWA B.747 N93106 at 0940 (TW770 from Chicago). South African Airways were making their first visit since October 1978, and the record number of ten wide-bodied aircraft on the ground at once was equalled again, but there were no first visits amongst them. (Mark White)

15th October 1979 – Two shots of N93106 (TW770), the first TWA B.747 to visit Manchester in the new colours. After a series of weekly flights to New York during the summer of 1978, the only visits by the airline until their demise in 2001 were diversions. (Both MA Archive via Ringway Publications)

15th October 1979 - Two shots of Boeing 747 G-AWNI (BA278), one of two British Airways B.747 diverts today, with the other being G-AWNH (BA260). Interestingly, five years after the formation of BA, they were still wearing a mixture of BA titles and tail colours, but the with old BOAC cheatline. In fact G-AWNI (above) and G-AWNK, which were both sold to TWA in early-1981 as N17125 & N17126 respectively, were still in the hybrid scheme when sold! (Both MA Archive via Ringway Publications)

15th October 1979 – This shot of Air India B747 VT-EBO (AI116) parked on stand 71, captures a totally different era, when health and safety was a lot less stringent. Note the open door towards the front of the aircraft that has neither steps attached, or any straps or barriers across it to prevent crew members or airport staff from having an unfortunate accident! (MA Archive via Ringway Publications)

17th November 1979 - Dense fog hitting many parts of England affected roads and caused delays and diversions, particularly at Heathrow. A morning diversion session produced nine, five of which were British Airways flights, L.1011 G-BEAL at 0633 (BA120 from Dhahran), 'endangered' SVC-10 G-ASGD at 0801 (BA058 from Larnaca) and B.747s G-AWNC (BA278 from Miami), G-AWNK (BA012 from Muscat) & G-BDPZ (BA299 from Chicago), which is showing signs of its recent lease to British Caledonian. (Geoff Ball)

17th November 1979 - South African Airways B.747 ZS-SAN 'Lebombo' arriving at 0905 (SA228 from Sal Island), on its second visit to Manchester, is seen here returning to Heathrow. Delivered in 1971, this aircraft had thirty-three years of continuous service with South African Airways. It is now preserved and on display at the SAA museum at Rand. (Geoff Ball)

17th November 1979 - Air India VT-EBE B.747 arriving at 0937 (AI110 from New York), was the last of today's diversions, and is seen here returning to Heathrow around lunchtime. The early morning mist and fog was about to be blown away, and replaced with wet and windy weather. (Geoff Ball)

17th November 1979 – The only first time visitor amongst today's nine diversions was Air New Zealand DC-10 ZK-NZT (BA270 from Boston). In May 1975 an agreement with the airline and BA enabled ANZ DC-10s to be flown by BA crew on the Heathrow-Los Angeles route, in place of BA's Boeing 707 aircraft. This lasted until March 1979, when British Airways returned to the route in their own right. ANZ DC-10s continued to be used on other BA routes, such as Miami, Toronto, Montreal and Boston. DC-10 ZK-NZT was the fifth of six different aircraft appearing at Manchester between 1975 and 1980. (Geoff Ball)

21st November 1979 – Yesterday, on the 20th November, Manchester was affected by dense freezing fog. The only four arrivals during the day, which all landed in the morning, were Dan-Air HS.748s G-BEBA (DA052) & G-ATMJ (DA053), along with Rockwell 690 D-IAFC and lastly, PA-34 Seneca G-BDUN.

Heathrow was also affected by fog yesterday up until late morning and again from early evening, when Prestwick alone received eleven wide-bodied aircraft! The first aircraft to land at Manchester today was not until 0953, but once the fog had started to lift, the airport was soon receiving fog diversions from Heathrow, which was affected until early evening. The first of these, British Airways BAC 1-11 G-AVMZ at 1105 (BA779 from Berlin), was followed in quick succession by Lear Jet HB-VFB, diverting into Manchester to pick up a passenger from the next flight to arrive, British Airways B.747 G-AWND at 1143 (BA278 from Miami). These were followed by a Gatwick diversion, Braniff B.747 N602BN (BN602 from Dallas), seen above shortly after arrival on its first visit to Manchester. (Mark White)

21ˢᵗ November 1979 – Following soon after the appearance of Braniff B.747, was Air New Zealand DC-10 ZK-NZM, arriving at 1207 (BA270 from Boston). Hot on its heels, was British Airways B.747s G-AWNK at 1211 (BA190 from Washington) & G-AWNF at 1229 (BA174 from New York). There was a temporary lull before the next diversions arrived which began with first time visitor Gulf Air Tristar L.1011 A4O-TZ at 1504, appearing in the fading light (GF007 from Doha). Apart from a couple of Birmingham diversions, Dan-Air BAC 1-11 G-BDAS (DA1537 from Malaga) and B.727 G-BAEF (DA1507 from Tenerife), the last Heathrow diversion to arrive at 1601 was British Airways SVC-10 G-ASGJ (BA150 from Cairo). This made a total of just eleven diversions, despite the London weather showing no improvement. By early evening, Liverpool had received three British Airways diversions, B.707 G-AXXZ (BA008 from Tokyo) and B.747s G-AWNB (BA018 from Frankfurt) & G-AWNP (BA012 from Prestwick) It was certain that at least two of these flights wanted to initially divert to Manchester, but were refused. One particularly interesting aircraft that also tried to divert to Manchester, but was unable to, was Singapore Airlines DC-10 9V-SDE, which was on delivery to the airline, routing through Heathrow. (John Harrington)

29th November 1979 – The month of November was officially described by the Met Office as 'unsettled and wet in the northwest'. Although this was true, it did not give the full picture. Despite all the wind and rain that was present, some foggy weather was produced on the 17th. Also, there was a particularly foggy period between the 21st and the 23rd. It was also recorded that a funnel cloud was spotted at Lossiemouth on the 15th, which is quite a rare phenomenon, and never forgotten if you happened to spot one! Today, the country was experiencing a mild spell, under a ridge of high pressure, centred over Africa with its winds blowing over the country originating back to Morocco. On waking up this morning, it felt quite warm, to the point where I opened my windows. I looked out and up at the clouds and noticed that they were high stratus clouds, tinged with orange. They looked rather strange and impressive at the same time, and later on, they provided a spectacular vibrant orange sunset. Another effect of this anticyclone was noticeable when using my aircraft radio. I noticed it could carry radio signals further than normal, and make weak signals that bit stronger. Throughout the day and much more prevalent after sunset, I could hear many more southern frequencies than normally audible. On a day that kept on giving, Heathrow suffered some fog briefly, but unfortunately most aircraft during this period diverted to Stansted. However, there were two diversions during the evening, the first of which was the only visit this year of Concorde, with the arrival of British Airways G-BOAD at 2052 (BA170 from New York), followed not long after by British Airways L.1011 G-BBAJ at 2105 (BA639 from Copenhagen). Overnight, Manchester experienced its warmest November since 1964, recording a temperature of 15°C. The following morning a thin layer of red sand, carried in the strong Saharan wind, had fallen to the ground and was covering most surfaces, and was especially noticeable on cars. (MA Archive via Ringway Publications)